WORKSHOP TIPS
& PROJECTS
FOR MODEL RAILROADERS

Cody Grivno

KALMBACH BOOKS

Kalmbach Books
21027 Crossroads Circle
Waukesha, Wisconsin 53186
www.Kalmbach.com/Books

Published in 2014
18 17 16 15 14   1 2 3 4 5

Manufactured in the United States of America

ISBN: 978-0-89024-869-0

Editor: Randy Rehberg
Art Director: Tom Ford
Illustrator: Rick Johnson
Photographers: Cody Grivno, Jim Forbes, Bill Zuback, Jeff Wilson, Paul Dolkos, and
Model Railroader staff

Publisher's Cataloging-In-Publication Data

Grivno, Cody.
   Workshop tips & projects for model railroaders / Cody Grivno.

      p. : col. ill. ; cm. -- (Model railroader books) -- (Modeling & painting series)

   Original projects previously published in Model Railroader magazine or on Cody's Office, the online video series.
   Issued also as an ebook.
   ISBN: 978-0-89024-869-0

   1. Railroads--Models--Handbooks, manuals, etc. 2. Railroads--Models--Design and construction. 3. Models and
modelmaking--Handbooks, manuals, etc. I. Title. II. Title: Workshop tips and projects for model railroaders
III. Series: Model railroader books.

TF197 .G758 2013
625.1/9

Dedication

This book is dedicated to my parents, Steve and Connie Grivno.

Dad, thanks for sharing your interest in trains (both model and full size), photography, and airbrushing with me. I will always cherish our daily trips to the Redland Yards in Crookston to see what the local had brought in.

Mom, thanks for supporting my love of trains. Whether it was being my driver to photograph trains before I had my license, visiting hobby shops, attending train shows, or stopping at railroad yards, you always did it with a smile.

Acknowledgements

This book is intended to provide modeling tips and techniques that will make your time at the workbench more enjoyable and productive. Think of this work as a "hybrid," as it features new content, as well as material that was previously published in *Model Railroader* magazine, with many of the ideas getting their start on "Cody's Office." I enjoy having modeling tips and information in one convenient source, and I hope this book fills that role for you.

I could not have written this book without the help of many individuals. Thanks to Dianne Wheeler, Randy Rehberg, Jeff Wilson, and Tom Ford from Kalmbach Books for giving me the opportunity to share these modeling tips and techniques with you, for editing my text (all typos can be blamed on our Siamese cat running across the keyboard), and for turning all the words and pictures into a cohesive package.

My coworkers at *Model Railroader* contributed material to this book and provided much encouragement. It's great to work with a group of guys who have such a strong passion for the hobby and enjoy sharing it with other enthusiasts.

Most importantly, thanks to my wife, Dorothy, and son, Albert, for their love and support during this process. I compiled much of this book after our toddler-age son went to bed, so my wife and I got to live college hours once again. Even though I'm more than 10 years removed from college, I was able to (with a few cans of soda along the way) make the hours between 11 p.m. and 2 a.m. a time of peak productivity.

Cody

Contents

Scenery

Painting and decaling

Weathering

TOOLS AND ADHESIVES

One key to successful and enjoyable model building is having the right tools and adhesives. In this section, we'll look at some of the basic tools that every modeler needs to get started, as well as some specialty items used in structure modeling.

In addition to tools, we'll examine a wide assortment of adhesives. Although you might think that all glues can be used interchangeably, they can't. There are specialized glues for plastic, wood, foam, and resin. In addition, I'll show you how to use a relatively new super glue designed specifically for acetal plastic, commonly used on locomotive handrails and for grab irons on freight cars.

Unlike tools, glues have a shelf life. I used to buy large bottles of cyanoacrylate adhesive, only to have them harden before I could use them up. Unless you're a prolific modeler, small- to medium-size bottles of glue will last you several months.

As we like to say at *Model Railroader*, "model railroading is fun." With the right tools and adhesives, the hobby will provide you many hours of enjoyment.

Put together a basic tool kit

Model railroading is a mechanically oriented pastime, and having the proper tools makes it much easier, **1**. I get the best tools I can afford, especially if I'll use them often. Proper hardening and manufacturing processes are often shortcut in cheap tools that can fail when you need them most.

Most hobby dealers sell tools, and they're also available online from Micro-Mark (micromark.com), Miniatronics (miniatronics.com), Trainworld (trainworld.com), Walthers (walthers. com), and other retailers.

Small tools are available from many different sources, and as long as you stick with the better quality tools, they'll work just fine.

Specialty tools

The hobby also employs various specialty tools. General Tools & Instruments (generaltools.com) makes the no. 1251 stainless steel model railroad reference rule and other useful items. Mascot Precision Tools, a division of Grobet USA, (grobetusa.com) offers an extensive selection of moderately priced modeler tools. X-acto (xacto.com) is known for its line of hobby knives and cutting tools. Xuron (xuron.com) makes numerous high-quality specialty pliers and cutters. And Wiha Quality Tools (wihatools.com) offers an extensive line of specialty screwdrivers, socket sets, and other tools in both English and metric sizes.

A cushioned bench cradle is handy for holding an inverted locomotive or car while you work on the wheels or couplers. Bowser and Ribbonrail make them for HO and N scales.

Coupler height gauges measure this important dimension to make sure the couplers function properly. Kadee (kadee.com) makes 10 different height

1

This look at a modeler's workbench shows many common hand tools and a few specialty items that most model railroaders use regularly.

gauges for HO, HOn3, O, On3, S, On2½, No. 1, and G scales. Micro-Trains (micro-trains.com) makes an N scale height gauge.

Coupler trip pin pliers are sold by Kadee and Micro-Mark. These pliers have a stepped round jaw and a curved opposing jaw to bend the trip pin without putting stress on the coupler.

A hobby knife with replaceable blades is a must for kit construction. X-acto offers numerous handles and blades for specific jobs. These knives are surgically sharp, so be sure to replace the blades regularly. A dull blade requires more cutting pressure, which makes it harder to control and is more dangerous than working with a sharp blade.

NMRA Standards gauges are available from the National Model Railroad Association in O, On3, On2½, Sn3, HO, HOn3, and N scales. These tools make it easy to check the accuracy of track components and wheelsets. Most hobby dealers sell them, and the gauges are available directly from nmra.org.

Needle files come in handy for all sorts of modeling jobs. I prefer the better quality sets from Micro-Mark, which last longer, don't load up, and are easy to clean with a brass brush.

Precision screwdrivers are available with either flat or Phillips reversible blades. Mascot and Wiha sell screwdriver sets in graduated sizes to provide the proper fit for any miniature screw.

Scale rules become more important as you begin to customize models and need to measure items in scale. General makes the most popular 12" rule, which is made of stainless steel with etched and blackened markings including N, HO, S, and O scale measurements. It also has scales divided into 64ths and millimeters, a table of decimal equivalents for number drills, and a table showing the tap and clearance drill sizes for small screws.

[Information on the needlenose pliers, sprue cutters, and other bending and cutting tools to include in your tool kit is found on the next page.]

Select tools that bend, grip, and cut

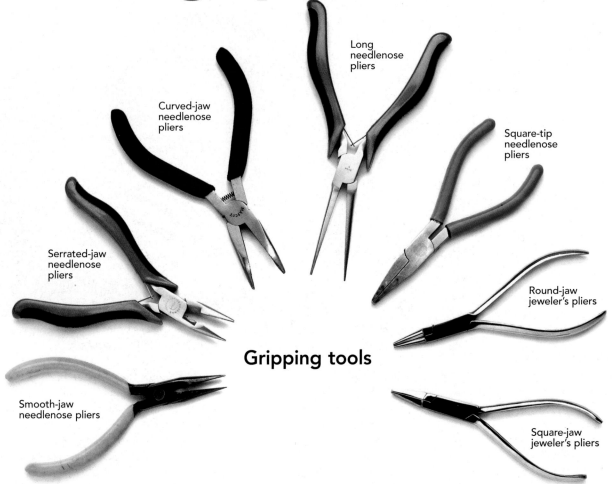

Long needlenose pliers

Curved-jaw needlenose pliers

Square-tip needlenose pliers

Serrated-jaw needlenose pliers

Round-jaw jeweler's pliers

Gripping tools

Smooth-jaw needlenose pliers

Square-jaw jeweler's pliers

Bending, gripping, and cutting are three of the most common tasks that any of us perform at our workbenches, and pliers can help with all three. A set of pliers meant for a specific task can make most jobs easier, so I keep quite a few pairs of modeling pliers and cutters handy when I'm working. My list may seem extravagant, but each tool has a different purpose, and the pliers are divided into gripping and cutting tools.

Gripping tools
Smooth-jaw needlenose pliers. These are my utility infielders, useful for bending light materials (though not

precisely) and gripping medium-size items. I like them a lot more now that I don't try to use them for everything because, while they're a multipurpose tool, they're not a universal tool.

Serrated-jaw needlenose pliers. These are useful when you need to hold something a bit more firmly and don't care if it gets a scratch or two, or for holding wire perpendicular to the jaws.

Curved-jaw needlenose pliers. You can use these for the same tasks as a standard pair of needlenose pliers but in those unusual situations where access is limited.

Long needlenose pliers. These look like needlenose pliers, but the extended tips are too delicate for most bending or forming jobs. I think of them as a pair of tweezers with a really comfortable handle, and that's how I use them.

Square-tip needlenose pliers. I love these pliers. The wide, flat jaws make them a bit stiffer, so they're good for situations where you need to grip items firmly. The square tips allow you to make precise bends in sheet metal.

Jeweler's pliers (two pairs). Use these tools for bending and forming small wire or thin sheet-metal parts. One pair has round jaws for forming small

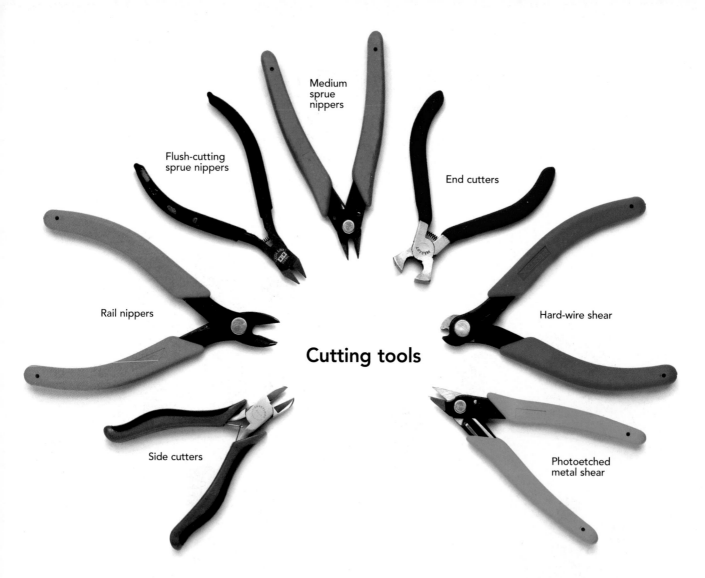

Medium sprue nippers

Flush-cutting sprue nippers

End cutters

Rail nippers

Cutting tools

Hard-wire shear

Side cutters

Photoetched metal shear

wire loops; the other pair has square jaws for forming flat metal strips. Other jaw shapes are available. They're great for fine bending and shaping but too light for anything else.

Cutting tools

Side cutters. These are the cutting equivalent of the needlenose pliers. They're good for general tasks, like wiring a layout or cutting brass wire, but because they're not flush cutters, they're a poor choice for cutting parts from sprue. Don't attempt to cut steel wire with them—you'll ruin their edges.

Rail nippers. These flush-cutting pliers are so handy that they make me wonder why I didn't get a pair 10 years ago. They're made to cut soft metal rail, but they also come in handy for cutting thick plastic sprues and styrene strips. However, only one side of a cut will be smooth and flush.

Flush-cutting sprue nippers. These cutters have smaller jaws than regular sprue nippers for finer, more precise work. They come in handy for trimming the smaller sizes of styrene strip. These can be hard to find in stores; mine are from Tamiya.

Medium sprue nippers. I use these to cut most plastic parts from sprues—exceptions are very small parts or really large ones. I use side cutters or rail nippers for the latter and then use a file for cleanup.

End cutters. Once in a while, you'll run into a task where you want to cut something off flush (a cast-on detail, for example). These are good for that task.

Hard-wire shear. I use these for (surprise!) cutting steel piano wire. Their jaws are hardened to do this job without damage.

Photoetched metal shear. I don't do a lot of work with thin, photoetched brass parts, but when I do, these fine shears are the tool I use. And I don't use them for anything else.

In addition, I keep several sizes of tweezers handy for gripping really small items, as well as a four-jawed screw starter and a small suction-cup gripper for working with windows. Smooth-tip tweezers are a good choice for decal application since they don't fracture the thin decal film.

The tools I have will handle most tasks I run into, but if I added any tools to my kit, they would probably be a pair of coupler-adjusting pliers (to shape air-hose actuating levers), a pair of combination tip pliers (one flat jaw opposing a round jaw), and perhaps a different style of flush-cutting shear.

Get a grip on glues and adhesives

White glue

Carpenter's wood glue

Contact cement

Construction adhesive

Five-minute epoxy

CA accelerator

Thick solvent cement

Solvent cement

Nontoxic solvent cement

Cyanoacrylate adhesive (CA)

CA debonder

Filler putty

An amazing array of adhesives and cements is available for use in model building and layout construction. The numerous kits and ready-to-run models available today contain a wide variety of materials including wood, metal, and plastic. It's important to choose the right adhesive to produce clean, secure bonds as you assemble your models.

I'll describe the most common adhesives and cements that modelers use. I'll also include a few special-purpose adhesives that come in handy for bonding unusual combinations of materials, as well as construction

adhesives that are useful in building layouts.

Always read the manufacturers' instructions and heed their safety warnings carefully, as some of these adhesives contain volatile solvents. Care must be taken to use them in a well-ventilated location away from any sources of ignition such as a gas furnace, water heater, or clothes dryer.

Solvent cement

Solvent cements are clear, watery liquid chemicals that are used to assemble plastic kits of all types. When using solvent cement, you'll want to dry-fit

the parts first. As you apply the liquid cement with a brush, the plastic parts soften and become "welded" together. There isn't any bulky residue after the cement evaporates, but avoid getting it on finished panels as the cement will etch and damage the surface. Some plastics require specific cements, so be careful to use the right solvent cement to obtain good bonds.

Thick solvent cement

These cements are clear, heavy-bodied liquids that come in a tube. Apply them along the edges of plastic surfaces to be joined before the parts are

GLUING PLASTICS

Four types of plastic are commonly used in modeling: ABS, acrylic, PVC, and styrene. Proper adhesives are needed to obtain strong joints.

ABS plastic is available in sheets, rods, strips, and molded detail parts. It is similar to styrene, but it's harder, more rigid, and a bit more brittle. ABS plastics require a clear, solvent-based cement. Fit the parts together and apply the cement along the joint so capillary action draws it into the joint. The cement softens the plastic and forms a chemical weld.

Acrylic is sold in sheets, shapes, rods, and tubing. Acrylic cement chemically welds the edges to make a strong joint.

PVC is available in solid sheets. You can also use plumbing pipe and fittings to simulate large tanks and pipelines. You can easily join PVC with solvent cement sold for use in plumbing work.

Styrene is the most popular modeling plastic. It has smooth surfaces, is easy to cut, and is sold in sheets, strips, rods, and shapes. It can be joined with commercial styrene cement. Apply the thin, watery types with a brush so capillary action draws the cement into the parts to produce a strong, chemically welded joint. The thick-bodied styrene cements are slower acting, which makes them useful for attaching details that require careful positioning.

brought together to make a welded joint. This type of cement dries slowly to allow you time to position and hold the parts in place.

Nontoxic solvent cement
A nontoxic solvent cement is a slower acting version of the more potent solvent cements, but it is much safer for use by young modelers.

Cyanoacrylate adhesive
Also known as super glue, cyanoacrylate adhesive (CA) comes in several viscosities with different setting times. Thin and medium viscosities work well for kit assembly, and can join parts made of dissimilar materials. However, thin CA sets almost instantly, and CA vapors can fog clear glazing and plated parts.

Thicker CA is slower acting, fills gaps, and allows more time for positioning parts before it sets up. Once the parts are held in place, a drop or two of chemical accelerator, applied with a micro brush, sets the joint almost instantly.

When working with CA, be sure to wear safety glasses and work in a well-ventilated area. Keep a bottle of debonder handy, as CA will bond skin instantly. In case of an accident, do not attempt to pull the skin bond apart. Instead, apply debonder and give it time to dissolve the adhesive.

Carpenter's wood glue
These common glues are part of a whole family of aliphatic resin glues with different setting and bonding characteristics useful for models made of wood, paper, and other porous materials.

White glue
White glue is a synthetic polyvinyl acetate emulsion adhesive that dries clear. At full strength, it's useful for bonding wood and similar materials. It's commonly thinned with water to apply scenery texturing materials.

Five-minute epoxy
This quick-acting epoxy is a two-part chemical adhesive that must be mixed thoroughly before application to produce exceptional strength. It's useful for bonding many dissimilar materials.

Filler putty
Filler putty is a thick-bodied adhesive used to fill gaps and seams. It comes in ready-to-use tubes or as a two-part epoxy that must be mixed to start the chemical reaction which produces its bonding strength. Both set slowly to allow time for application and shaping.

Contact cement
Contact cements, such as Barge Cement, Gorilla Glue, Pliobond, and Walthers Goo, are rubbery plastic adhesives that grab on contact to bond dissimilar materials. Once bonded, they resist shock. Most contact cements contain solvents that may attack some plastic materials.

Some contact cements come as liquid adhesives made for brush application or in spray cans. These adhesives are most commonly used to fasten sheets of printed texturing material on walls or to fasten detail elements to a backdrop. The adhesive is applied in a thin layer to both surfaces and then it's allowed to dry. Once the cement dries, the two surfaces must be carefully aligned without touching, as once contact is made, the bond is instantaneous and permanent.

Construction adhesive
Construction adhesives such as DAP clear or gray adhesive caulk (dap.com), Liquid Nails Projects & Foamboard Adhesive no. LN-604 (liquidnails.com), and Loctite PL300 Foamboard Adhesive (loctiteproducts.com) are sold in cartridges for application with a caulking gun. They don't attack extruded foam insulation board, produce a strong bond overnight, and clean up with water before the bond cures. In addition, a thin layer of adhesive caulk is useful for securing roadbed and flextrack during layout construction.

All of these products require clean and dry contact surfaces, free of dust, to produce the strongest bonds. Tight and carefully fitted parts also contribute to joint strength, especially with cyanoacrylate adhesives. And don't forget that large modeling projects can be reinforced with concealed strips of styrene or wood to prevent warping and provide additional strength.

Glue structures using braces and jigs

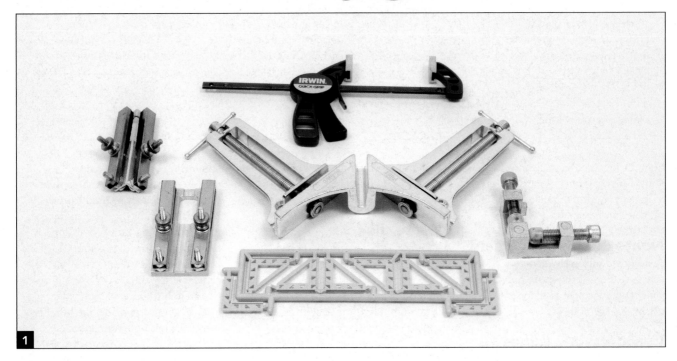

1

Building structure kits is one of the most enjoyable activities of model railroading. There are hundreds of buildings available in a variety of mediums, including plastic, laser-cut wood, brass, and resin. The key to making the kits look their best is having straight wall joints that are free of gaps. Fortunately, a variety of clamps and jigs make this possible, **1**.

Miniature bar clamps, such as the 4" Irwin Quick-Grip, are ideal for holding wall sections together for gluing, **2**. The clamps work best on kits with thicker walls, such as those offered by Smalltown USA and Design Preservation Models (DPM). Irwin offers its Quick-Grip bar clamps in other sizes, which are suitable for larger buildings and benchwork. Designed primarily for the construction trade, bar clamps can be found at hardware stores and home-supply centers.

Just down the aisle from the bar clamps, you'll most likely find corner clamps. The one shown in photo **3** is

Clamps and braces make structure assembly easier. Shown clockwise from bottom are City Classics corner braces, the Splice Clamp and Right Clamp from Coffman Graphic Solutions, Irwin's Quick-Grip, and a Panavise right-angle clamp. In the middle is Pony's corner clamp.

made by Pony and designed for holding parts at right angles. The firm also makes adjustable corner clamps for holding parts at other angles. Because the clamp uses metal construction, you'll want to put cardboard between the jaws of the clamp and the parts you're working on.

Hobby-specific clamps include the Right Clamp and the newer Splice Clamp, which are offered by Coffman Graphic Solutions. The Right Clamp is available in various sizes for holding wall sections at 90-degree angles, **4**. The metal clamps feature foam pads for protecting the model's surface and a window for applying glue. The clamp's opening is adjusted with two thumbscrews.

The Splice Clamp uses the same construction features but is designed

for butt joints, **5**. The clamp is ideal if you're assembling modular wall panels, such as those sold by Rix Products, DPM, and Wm. K. Walthers.

For smaller projects, Panavise sells clamps that hold parts at 90-degree angles, **6**. The clamps also use thumbscrews and have padded ends to protect the model from being marred. The clamp is handy for holding small details in HO scale as well as N and Z structure walls.

City Classics recently introduced injection-molded plastic braces (no. 209) for reinforcing corner joints and keeping them at a right angle. A 16-pack includes 12 braces for inside corners and 4 for outside corners, **7**.

No matter what scale you model in, there are clamps for virtually all sizes of structures.

2 Irwin's 4" Quick-Grip bar clamp holds the glue joint tight on this Smalltown USA kit. This clamp and larger versions are also handy for assembling benchwork.

3 Pony's corner clamp, used primarily by picture frame makers and woodworkers, can also be used to hold parts at a 90-degree angle. The clamps use all-metal construction, which can damage plastic and other soft materials. Protect your work by setting cardboard between the clamp's jaws and the model's parts.

4 The Right Clamp, produced by Coffman Graphic Solutions, is designed for holding wall sections at a right angle. Foam pads protect the model, and small windows allow glue to be applied inside the joint.

5 Assembling modular walls is easy with the Splice Clamp, also produced by Coffman Graphic Solutions. The two thumbscrews are used to adjust the clamp's jaws.

6 If you model in smaller scales, Panavise makes this clamp that keeps parts at a right angle. The pads at the end of the screws keep the metal from marring parts.

7 Corner braces from City Classics help reinforce corner joints and keep walls square. Each pack includes braces for inside and outside corners.

TRACK AND WIRING

Although Kalmbach Books offers several great titles covering track and wiring, I'd be remiss if I didn't include a bit of information on these topics. In this section, I've picked a sampling of one-evening projects from the pages of *Model Railroader* that cover the basics of track laying and wiring.

Wiring and soldering are two tasks that many modelers dread. In this section, you'll learn how to solder wire and track feeders, use connectors to make layout wiring easier, and even wire a layout for two-train operation.

In addition, you'll learn some of senior editor Jim Hediger's techniques for laying track and improving commercial turnouts. Jim's HO scale Ohio Southern is one of the best running layouts I've ever seen, and his advice comes from more than 50 years of experience in the hobby.

Ballast track easily

Use a paintbrush to spread the ballast between the rails and move any granules off the ties.

Wet the ballast with 70 percent isopropyl alcohol and let it soak in for a minute before adding Scenic Cement.

Apply gentle pressure to the pipette, so the granules wouldn't wash out when adding the Scenic Cement.

When the Scenic Cement is visible between the granules, you know the ballast is thoroughly saturated.

On *Model Railroader*'s Beer Line project layout, which was set in 1947 Milwaukee, I ballasted the track on the entire layout using a favorite technique.

I used a 50:50 blend of Highball Products Light Gray and Dark Gray limestone ballast, which looks similar to ballast used by the Milwaukee Road. I mixed the ballast in a half-gallon ice cream bucket (after I'd eaten the ice cream), which was more than enough for our 4 x 12-foot layout.

However, I didn't stop with the gray ballast. I used Highball Products cinders on some sidings and along the edge of the right-of-way.

I ballasted between the rails first. I used a ½"-wide paintbrush to spread the granules, **1**. Then I dragged the

brush back and forth until there was no ballast on the tops of the ties.

I wet the ballast with 70 percent isopropyl alcohol, **2**. The alcohol makes it easier for the Woodland Scenics Scenic Cement to wick between the granules by breaking the surface tension of the water-based glue.

I let the alcohol soak in for a minute and then applied Scenic Cement with a pipette, **3**. To prevent the granules from washing out between the ties, I applied gentle pressure to the pipette.

I let the ballast dry overnight and began work on the shoulders. I mixed some thinned white glue (80 percent glue, 20 percent water). I used a second ½"-wide paintbrush to spread the glue along the shoulder of the roadbed, keeping an even edge along the base.

I sprinkled a layer of ballast into the wet glue. Once the glue had dried, I cleaned up the loose granules with a vacuum. Then, I used a spoon to apply a second coat of ballast. I shaped the ballast along the beveled edge of the cork roadbed with a 1"-wide foam brush. I used the same technique to apply the cinders along the edge of the ballast.

With the ballast shaped, I sprayed the granules with 70 percent isopropyl alcohol and let it soak in. Then I applied Scenic Cement in two steps. I first placed a pipette against the outside web of the rail and let the cement trickle down. Next, I dragged the pipette along the bottom edge of the ballast and let the cement wick up, **4**. When I could see Scenic Cement between the granules, the ballast was thoroughly saturated.

Work with curved turnouts

1 On the HO scale Ohio Southern layout, three Peco curved turnouts are used to fit in a reverse loop staging yard. The switch machines are top mounted for easier maintenance and clearance underneath.

The smooth-flowing lines of a gently curved switch lead produce some of the most realistic looking trackwork you're likely to find. For many years, handlaying the track was the only option for modelers who wanted to capture this appearance. But in recent years, track manufacturers have responded to the demand for ready-to-use curved turnouts.

Curved turnouts are special switches that join two tracks curving in the same direction. Prototype railroads have these switches built to fit specific locations where a regular turnout won't work.

Uses for curved turnouts

Modelers have a more limited selection of curved turnouts, but once you catch on to how they work, you'll find many uses for them. On my own HO scale Ohio Southern, I've used them to help compress leads into my staging yards, lengthen passing tracks, provide crossovers on curves, smooth the entry into the last tracks in yard ladders, and fit industrial spurs into tight locations.

The reverse loop staging yard that represents my upper deck Virginian & Ohio connection is the first location where I used a group of Peco curved turnouts, **1**. The entry side of the yard is straight, so I used three regular medium radius (equivalent to no. 5) turnouts to serve the four tracks.

As the staging tracks loop around, they return to the lead track at almost a 45-degree angle that's far too sharp for normal turnouts. I wound up using a regular medium left at the junction with the straight entry lead and added three SL-87 Code 100 Universal double-radius left-hand turnouts to blend the staging tracks into the exit turnout.

There are other potential applications for using curved turnouts, **2**. The ones with larger radii come in handy to lengthen passing tracks by placing them in an end curve well before the track straightens out.

Used in pairs, curved turnouts can be combined to make crossovers in double-tracked curves. I've had excellent results with a long curved crossover leading into my main yard from the south. It provides access to the main yard for setouts and pickups by through trains. I used Walthers no. 8 curved turnouts in this location, and they're now going on more than 25 years of service.

The end of a yard ladder is another place where a medium-size curved turnout can smooth the entry into the last pair of tracks. When I used all straight turnouts in my ladders, I always wound up with a fairly sharp curve where the last track was bent to run parallel with the rest of the yard. Now I use a Peco double-curved turnout in this location,

CURVED TURNOUT APPLICATIONS

Extend a passing siding

Curved turnout

Normal turnout location

Curved crossovers

Right hand

Right hand

Left hand

Left hand

End of a yard ladder

Curved turnout
makes gentler curves

Industry inside a curve

2

You can use curved turnouts to extend a passing siding, make crossovers in double-tracked curves, smooth entry at the end of a yard ladder, and cut an industry track into the inside of a mainline curve.

CURVED TURNOUTS

HO SCALE

BK Enterprises   troutcreekeng.com
- Kits for curved turnouts with shaped points and rails (without ties)

Peco   peco-uk.com
- Code 100 Setrack line double-radius
- Code 100 Universal line double-radius
- Code 83 (U.S.) Streamline no. 7 double-radius (Electrofrog or Insulfrog)
- Code 75 Streamline double-radius

Walthers   walthers.com
- Code 83 double-curved no. 6½, no. 7, no. 7½, and no. 8

N SCALE

Atlas   atlasrr.com
- Code 55 curved

BK Enterprises   troutcreekeng.com
- Kits for curved turnouts with shaped points and rails (without ties)

Peco   peco-uk.com
- Code 55 medium-radius double-curved
- Code 80 double-curved (Electrofrog or Insulfrog)

so the curves into the last two tracks are wider and operate better.

Finally, I've used an occasional curved turnout to cut an industry track into the inside of a mainline curve. I've always liked the looks of a track curving along the outside of an older building.

Installing the turnouts

As I began installing my first curved crossover, I realized that good alignment was going to be critical anywhere large locomotives and heavy traffic abound.

When I install curved turnouts, I do a lot of leaning down and sighting along the rails to make sure the curve continues smoothly and that there aren't any kinks at the rail joints. To install a crossover, I cut in the outside turnout first and slide the rail joiners in place to hold it. I position the inside turnout and make sure it's aligned through the crossover before I cut it into the inside curve. Then, I make any minor adjustments needed to align the inside curves.

I've learned that bigger locomotives tend to naturally find any imperfections in the outer curved rails, especially at rough rail joints. I also carefully sharpen the curved switch points with a file to get a smooth transition before installation. I test my switch points by sliding a thumbnail along the inside of the railheads to find any rough spots.

Ribbonrail track alignment gauges come in handy to ensure that all of the rails curve uniformly through the turnouts and the approach tracks. Then I solder the rail joints within the installation to secure everything before final spiking.

Use magnetic couplers

Kadee introduced its Magne-Matic HO coupler in 1959, and it became the virtual standard. When the expiration of Kadee's patents allowed other companies to market similar magnetic knuckle couplers, they became original equipment in most ready-to-run and kit rolling stock. However, the majority of model railroad operators simply ignore magnetic uncoupling and uncouple their cars manually.

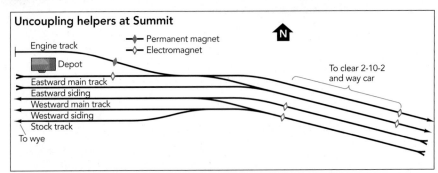

I installed electromagnets under ties of the eastward main line and siding and a concealed permanent magnet under the engine track.

Uncoupling for operators

Manual uncoupling is nonetheless completely understandable from an operator's perspective. After all, even in the high-tech environment of today's railroads, a crew person still has to lift or pull an uncoupling lever handle to separate cars, trains, and locomotives. In some respect, then, manual uncoupling approximates a basic part of a professional railroader's everyday job.

It's also true that manual uncoupling frees layout builders from some planning. If you want to use concealed magnets to uncouple, you have to think through possible switching movements in advance to decide where to install the uncouplers as you lay the track. This can be a daunting prospect for builders inexperienced in operation, and more trouble than many think it's worth.

Expense and complexity are concerns too. For layouts with many switching locations, the cost of magnets adds up, especially where electromagnets are needed to prevent accidental uncouplings. And for simpler shelf switching layouts or any with all track within easy reach, there may be no reason to complicate the construction or wiring.

Uncoupling helpers

Magnetic uncoupling does have applications, and more builders might want to consider them. The diagram shows part of the Summit, Calif., track arrangement on my HO scale Cajon Pass layout. Helper service was a major part of the 1947 mainline Santa Fe and Union Pacific operations I want to model, and this station at the top of the pass is where helpers cut off the trains to return downhill to their base in San Bernardino.

There was a regularity to the helpers' movements, including where and how they were separated from the trains they helped. When eastward passenger trains had helpers, they double-headed in front of the road engines. Arriving at Summit, a passenger train with a helper stopped on the eastward main west of the engine track switch and uncoupled the helper engine, so it could run ahead and back into the engine track behind the depot.

On eastward freights, the helpers were cut in as pushers ahead of the way car (caboose). After stopping east of the crossover, on either the eastward main or siding, the pushers uncoupled from their trains, backed their way cars onto the engine track, and then left the way car on a grade there while they moved into the clear toward the depot on the eastward main. The crew would line the engine track switch and let the way car roll out of the inclined track back to the train. If the way car didn't coast far enough, the helper was now behind it and could shove it to a coupling.

Freight or passenger helpers then worked their way over to the stock track using crossovers west of the depot. The stock track led to the wye, where the engines turned to face west for the trip home.

Installing electromagnets

With these regular movements in mind, I installed electromagnets concealed under the ties of the eastward main line and eastward siding, and a concealed permanent magnet under the engine track. I also installed electromagnets under the westward main line and siding where doubleheading helpers on westbound trains would cut off.

Part of what makes these uncoupling magnets worthwhile is that Summit is 66" above the floor, and even when standing on a 10"-high operating platform, it can be awkward to reach across three or four tracks at that height. Eventually, I'll add details like switch stands and line poles to the scene, so I'd rather operators didn't reach in at all. Magnetic uncoupling will make that possible, and will add a bit of unseen magic to the train and engine movements at Summit.

My five electromagnets are powered by a time-delay circuit. I use a five-position rotary switch to select which magnet will be energized when the button is pushed. The magnets stay powered long enough to let the helper engineers get both hands back on the throttle to complete the uncoupling movement.

There are other situations where magnetic uncoupling can pay off. I plan to use electromagnets on double-ended freight yard tracks, so yard engineers can work from chairs.

Magnetic knuckle couplers gives us a capability for action at a distance. It's too good an opportunity to overlook.

Tune up turnouts

1 Use an NMRA gauge to check turnouts and make any necessary adjustments before installing them on your layout.

Blunt point

2 Some commercial turnouts have blunt points that can catch wheel flanges and cause derailments.

Sharpened point

3 File the blunt points so they fit flush against the stock rail.

4 Running your thumbnail along the rail allows you to easily detect points that still need some filing. If your nail catches, the point needs some adjustment.

Many modelers build their layouts with commercial turnouts with the expectation that these components are ready to install. However, building my HO Ohio Southern has convinced me that most commercial turnouts are really "ready to finish." They may need a little tune-up to ensure smooth performance and reliable operation.

Gauge (the proper spacing of the rails) is critical throughout, and anything that impedes the smooth passage of the wheels is a potential problem. I use an NMRA gauge to check these items on my turnouts, **1**.

Where the track gauge is too tight, it squeezes the flanges between the railheads, forcing the wheels to climb up and derail. If the gauge is too wide, the wheelsets can't span the extra distance between the guardrails and the frog, which forces the wheels to bounce up and again leads to derailment.

Most of the turnouts I've used tend to be a bit wide at the frog. I correct this by using a needle file to remove material from the inside faces of the guardrail and the frog until the gauge pins fit properly. I sharpen the point of the frog at this time as well.

I use a flat needle file to sharpen the movable switch points. Manufactured points tend to have blunt ends that can catch wheel flanges, **2**, so I file each point to a gentle taper that fits tightly against the stock rail, **3**. To provide a smooth passage for the wheels, I also taper the top edge of the point. If you can slide a fingernail over this transition without it snagging, the wheels will also pass the point easily, **4**.

These steps take only a few minutes, but they pay off big time with problem-free operation, which makes running trains that much more fun.

Use connectors for easier layout wiring

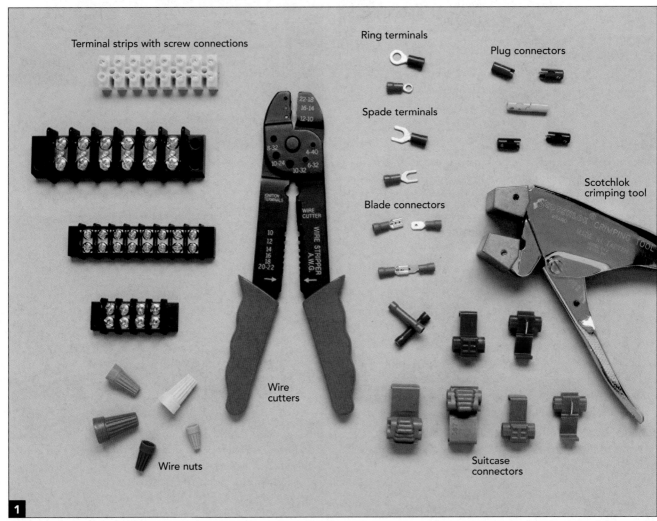

Terminal strips with screw connections

Ring terminals

Plug connectors

Spade terminals

Scotchlok crimping tool

Blade connectors

Wire cutters

Wire nuts

Suitcase connectors

1

A wide range of connectors can come in handy during the wiring of a model railroad. Most are sold by hardware stores and home centers.

Connectors are mechanical devices used to join the wires in electrical circuits. These connectors may be plugs, like the ones used between modules in portable layouts, or they may be a more permanent connection that's made using a crimping tool during assembly. Most don't require soldering.

Electrical hardware is sold under dozens of brand names, and there are hundreds of connectors to choose from, **1**. Most connectors are designed to do specific jobs ranging from joining single wires to connecting groups of wires or a cable. Let's take a look at some of the common connectors that are useful for model railroad applications.

Terminal strips

Terminal strips, also called *terminal blocks*, are one of the first electrical additions to most model railroads because they provide a handy way to connect wires in an organized fashion. They're also built into most of the electrical control components used in layout control systems.

Each terminal strip has a row of electrical connections, or terminals, mounted on an insulated base. The most common strips use screw terminals to secure the wire connections without soldering, and some have insulated barriers separating the terminals.

The barrier strips are often used with ring or spade terminals crimped onto the wires.

Screw terminals offer a simple connection for two or more wires. However, if you aren't using wire terminals, be careful to wrap all of the wires around the screws in a clockwise direction. This helps to hold the wires in place as the screw is tightened down.

Terminal strips are available in many different lengths to provide enough terminals for any job. They also have different terminal sizes to accommodate various wire sizes. Some have contacts with screws along both ends, others have only soldering tabs, and some have combination terminals with screws along one side and soldering tabs on the other. I've found the latter combination works great inside control panels, as I wire them on the workbench with soldered connections. Once the panel is mounted on the layout, I use the screw terminals to make the connections to the railroad.

Any wire connected to a terminal strip must have a short length of its insulation stripped off. This is easy to do with a wire stripping tool, but care is required to avoid nicking the wire, which may cause a break when the wire flexes.

A little advance planning is required to protect the terminal strip from contact with fingers or foreign objects. Model railroads using Digital Command Control (DCC) may deliver enough current to cause burns, and finger contact may cause problems with sensitive electronic detection circuits.

Terminal strips are sold by hardware stores, most electrical suppliers, electronics stores, and hobby dealers.

Crimp-on terminals

Crimp-on terminals are available in many sizes and types to provide neater wiring connections, especially with stranded wire. These connectors secure all of the tiny wire strands to prevent short circuits. In some cases, the wires may also be soldered to the connectors.

Ring terminals are commonly used where multiple wires must connect to a single terminal. The ring termi-

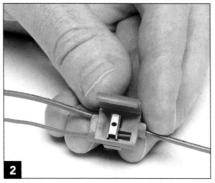

2

Insulation-displacement connectors connect wires without having to strip off insulation. The connector's knife cuts through the insulation to connect the conductors.

nal requires complete removal of the terminal screw to make or break its connection.

A spade terminal has an open end, so it can easily slip under a loosened terminal screw. This makes the installation or removal of a single wire connection easy.

Blade connectors have a flat metal tongue that's inserted into a similar flat receptacle with clips along both sides. Because of the pull required to separate these connectors, the wires are often soldered into both components.

Crimp-on terminals and crimping pliers are sold by auto parts stores, hardware retailers, and electronics stores. They're available in sets and as refill packs of single-size terminals.

Plug connectors

An ideal electrical plug connector should have excellent internal contacts, resist vibration and disconnect pressure, be easy to connect or disconnect, and have some means of orienting the plugs. The plug may carry one or multiple circuits. For portable layouts, compact size, durability, rapid assembly, low cost, and easy identification are also important characteristics.

Standard grounded plugs are necessary for any power circuits that handle 110V line voltage.

Some printed-circuit boards have built-in miniature plugs which allow them to be disconnected from the wires. This arrangement is often found in DCC decoder and sound system installations. Some decoders also

have quick release connectors for easy removal.

Wire nuts are single connectors for two or three wires. They're often used to wire household light fixtures and come in sizes that match different wire sizes.

To use a wire nut, the wires must be stripped so the bare ends can be twisted tightly together in a clockwise direction. When the proper size wire nut is applied and tightened down, the wires will be secure and insulated. Any bare conductors should be covered by the apron of the wire nut.

Wire nuts are available from home centers and hardware stores.

Insulation-displacement connectors

Insulation-displacement connectors are special devices introduced by 3M 45 years ago to speed up the wiring process, **2**. These metal and plastic connectors eliminate the time-consuming need to strip insulation from the wires. Electricians have nicknamed them *suitcase connectors* due to their shape when closed.

Insulation-displacement connectors (IDCs) have metal, U-shaped slotted tabs called knives inside their plastic cases. After the wires are set in position, the IDC's knife is squeezed tight with a pair of pliers to drive the metal through the insulation and connect the conductors within the slots. Then the plastic case is closed to insulate the connection.

Special pliers are available from 3M to evenly apply the force to make a perfect connection. However, less expensive tools can also do a good job, such as Robo-Grip cam-action pliers and Channellock pliers. Common pliers can also be used with acceptable results.

These IDCs are often used to add accessories to automobile wiring. They're especially useful for DCC wiring where a track feeder is being connected to the main power bus. There are competitors, but we've had the best results with Scotchlok IDCs.

The IDCs and the crimping pliers are sold by some auto supply stores, electrical suppliers, home centers, and Micro-Mark.

Wire a layout for two-train operation

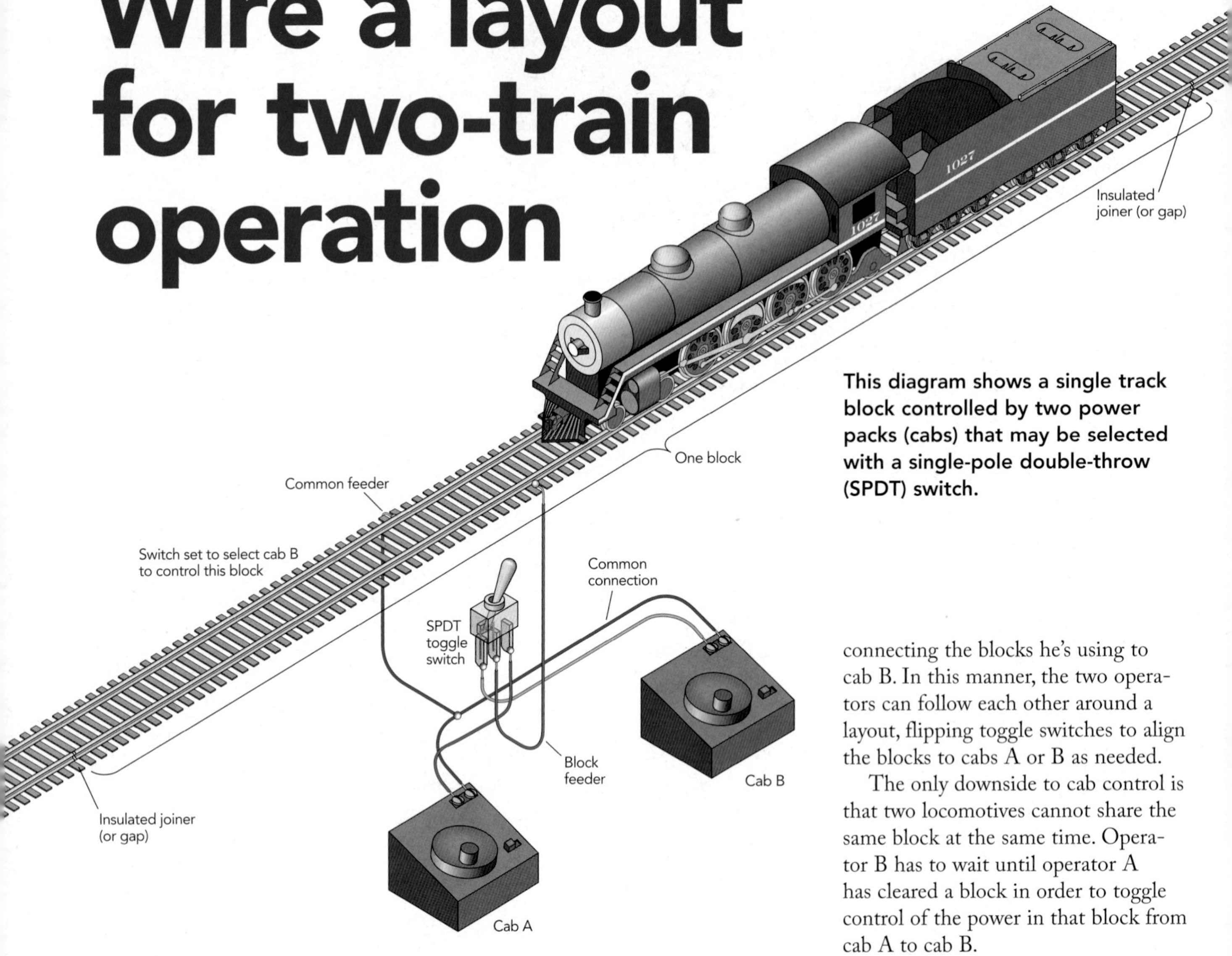

Insulated joiner (or gap)

One block

Common feeder

Switch set to select cab B to control this block

SPDT toggle switch

Common connection

Block feeder

Cab B

Insulated joiner (or gap)

Cab A

This diagram shows a single track block controlled by two power packs (cabs) that may be selected with a single-pole double-throw (SPDT) switch.

With two direct-current power packs, single-pole double-throw (SPDT) toggle switches, and hardware-store wire, you can divide any layout into electrical blocks that will allow two trains to be operated independently.

How it works

With cab control wiring, a layout using two power packs is divided into several electrically isolated sections called *blocks*. Each block is independent of the others, so a train in block A can be operated by power pack A, and a train in block B can be run by power pack B.

Each block starts and ends with a plastic insulated rail joiner or a narrow gap cut through the metal rails. So

while a cab control layout visually looks like a continuous track, electrically, it's several independent track sections that line up with one another at each end.

As an operator using power pack A moves his locomotive through one block and approaches the next block, he uses a toggle switch to connect the second block to power pack A (or cab A). Now, the two blocks are electrically united to cab A and the locomotive seamlessly moves from the first block to the second. Just before he enters a third block, he connects the new block to cab A. Following this pattern, the operator can move his locomotive from one end of a layout to the other.

While this is occurring, a second operator using cab B can operate his locomotive elsewhere on the layout by

connecting the blocks he's using to cab B. In this manner, the two operators can follow each other around a layout, flipping toggle switches to align the blocks to cabs A or B as needed.

The only downside to cab control is that two locomotives cannot share the same block at the same time. Operator B has to wait until operator A has cleared a block in order to toggle control of the power in that block from cab A to cab B.

SPDT electrical switches can connect only one cab to a block at a time, so there's no way for both operators to connect their power packs to the same block at the same time. The only way to get into trouble is to run a train across the insulated rail joiners into another block connected to the other cab, so it's important for operators to know exactly where one block ends and the next begins.

Blocks and wiring

A layout, at minimum, needs three blocks for two trains, but more blocks give operators more flexibility. Figure **1** shows wiring for a simple oval layout with one passing siding that's been divided into five electrical blocks. Each block is controlled by its own SPDT toggle switch.

Some SPDT switches have a center off position that doesn't connect power in either direction. This is especially useful for passing sidings (and spurs), since it allows you to cut power in that track to park a train.

It's also smart to turn a block off after your train departs, or the next train that enters the block will be controlled by the wrong cab.

Each block has a feeder wire connecting it to an SPDT switch. If a layout has six blocks it will need six SPDT switches.

When making track blocks, you need to insulate or cut a gap in just one rail. Think of a light switch in your house. When you turn a lamp on or off, you interrupt only one of the wires that lead to the lamp, not both.

In cab control wiring, the rail that isn't insulated or cut is called the *common rail*. This rail gets connected to both power packs (see the blue wire in figure 1). While connecting two power packs in this manner may cause a bit of anxiety for a model railroader new to electricity, trust me, it works.

Also, by using a common rail, you save on wire, toggle switches, and soldering, since you'll need to purchase only SPDT switches instead of the more expensive double-pole double-throw (DPDT) switches.

Atlas Selectors

An alternative to toggle switches are Atlas Selectors, which are banks of four SPDT switches designed specifically for model railroads, and using them doesn't require soldering, **2**.

The Atlas no. 215 Selector is an inexpensive set of four single-pole double-throw slide switches for model railroad applications. Each selector has screw connections and can be used with two power packs to operate four blocks. Selectors are designed to be used in multiples, so any number can be easily connected side-by-side (called *ganging*) to control any number of blocks.

Like SPDT toggle switches, selectors have three positions: a connection to power pack A, a center off position, and a connection to power pack B. Selectors are even labeled A and B.

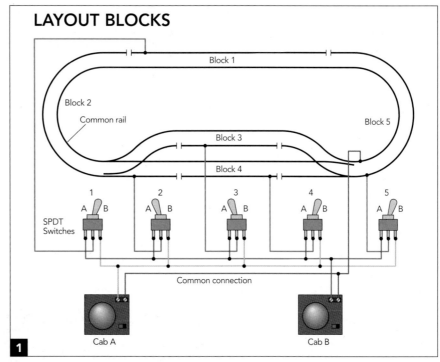

LAYOUT BLOCKS

1

This diagram shows cab control wiring for an oval layout with a passing siding (block 3), four other blocks, and two cabs.

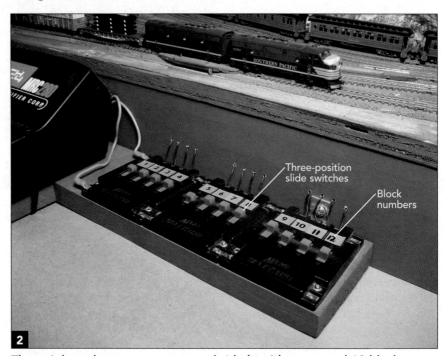

2

Three Atlas selectors are connected side by side to control 12 blocks on this small N scale cab control layout.

Atlas also makes a companion device called the no. 220 Connector, which contains three on/off single-pole single-throw switches in the same housing.

Power packs

The easiest way to build a cab control layout is by using a pair of identical DC power packs. Figure 1 shows how to connect one track terminal from each power pack to the common rail on your layout. Keep in mind that your track configuration may shift the common rail from the inside of your layout to the outside. Follow the rail around your layout with your finger to be sure

CAB CONTROL TERMS

Block: A section of track on a layout that is electrically isolated from adjoining sections by use of plastic rail joiners or gaps cut in rails. Blocks can be any length—usually determined by a specific track plan.

Block switch: A single-pole double-throw electrical switch that's used to connect one wire to either of two other wires. While most hobbyists think of toggle switches, slide and rotary switches can also have SPDT contacts. Some SPDT toggle switches are made with a center off position that does not connect to either wire.

Cab: Another name for a direct current power pack with speed and direction controls to operate a train.

Cab control wiring: A method of wiring a model railroad using two or more power packs and track electrical blocks to allow independent operation of two or more trains.

Common rail: An electrically continuous rail that connects both power packs to complete the common electrical circuit. The other rail is called the *control rail* in which gaps are cut to define the electrical blocks.

Feeder: The wire connecting a segment of rail to the power supply.

Insulated rail joiner: A rail joiner made of an insulating material such as plastic instead of metal.

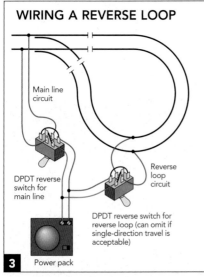

WIRING A REVERSE LOOP

Main line circuit

DPDT reverse switch for main line

Reverse loop circuit

DPDT reverse switch for reverse loop (can omit if single-direction travel is acceptable)

Power pack

3

This diagram shows the wiring needed to connect a DC reverse loop to a single power pack.

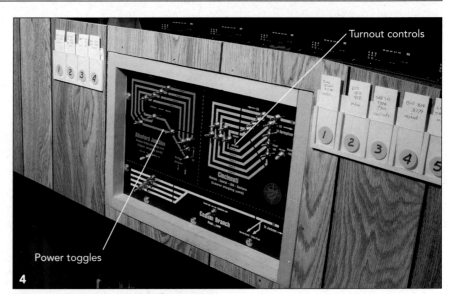

Turnout controls

Power toggles

4

Miniature toggle switches in this compact DC panel control two reverse loop staging yards and one stub-ended yard on Jim Hediger's HO scale Ohio Southern.

you have correctly identified the common rail so that you don't break or "gap" it by mistake.

If you're using two different power packs and mix up your wiring, it'll create a short circuit and activate the power packs' circuit breakers to cut power until the short is fixed. Don't worry, though. As the breakers cool, they'll automatically restore the power once the short is fixed.

Wiring a reverse loop

Any track configuration that permits a train to change its direction without simply backing up needs a special electrical circuit to prevent a short. Wiring

a reverse loop, wye, or turntable may seem similar to block wiring, but there are some important differences.

Basic reverse-loop wiring for a direct current layout requires double-pole double-throw toggle switches to change the polarity of the two rails in the reverse loop and in the track block preceding the loop, **3**. These DPDT switches allow an engineer to align the polarity of the rails so his train may enter or exit the reverse loop without causing a short circuit as it passes over the insulated rail joints.

If a train enters a track wye to turn around, insulated joints and a similar combination of two DPDT switches

are needed to align the polarity so the train may leave the wye.

Simple or complex

Cab control wiring can be as simple as in figure 1, or it can use many more blocks and power packs to let additional operators connect to a specific group of blocks on a large layout. The complex, color-coded control panel shown in photo **4** operates three different staging yards.

Cab control of model railroads has been around for decades, and it's the best way to move from a single loop layout to more complex operation, short of entering the world of Digital Command Control.

Shape and install spike-head feeders

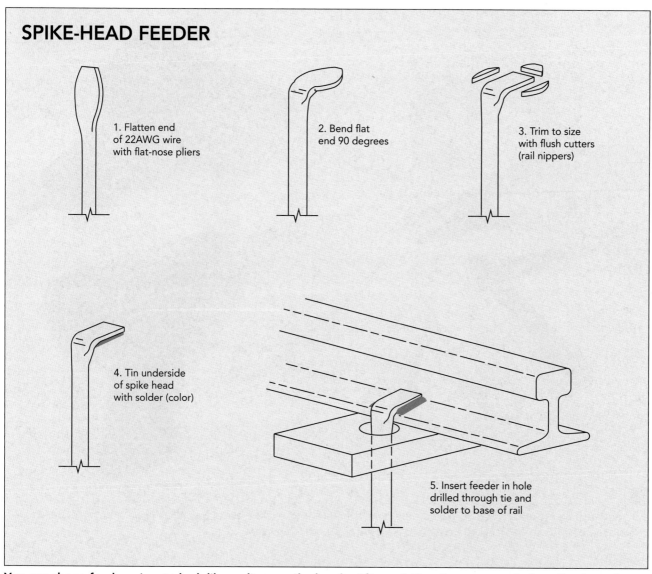

SPIKE-HEAD FEEDER

1. Flatten end of 22AWG wire with flat-nose pliers

2. Bend flat end 90 degrees

3. Trim to size with flush cutters (rail nippers)

4. Tin underside of spike head with solder (color)

5. Insert feeder in hole drilled through tie and solder to base of rail

You can shape feeder wires to look like ordinary spike heads. After painting them to match the rails, the spike heads, which are not much larger than the heads of track spikes, blend into the trackwork.

If your goal is to build a layout for realistic operations, the number one requirement is that it works reliably. One way I'm achieving that on my HO layout is to run an electrical feeder to every piece of rail, with short, direct connections to the Digital Command Control (DCC) bus wires. This guarantees a solid current path and avoids problems caused by voltage drop in

long runs of rail or by faulty connections at rail joints.

For years, I made feeder connections with a wire bent into a sort of dogleg and dropped through a hole drilled between two ties next to the base of the rail. However, I was afraid that a lot of them—one on every piece of rail—would detract from the appearance of my handlaid trackwork.

My friend Perry Squier had the same concern and started shaping the feeder wires on his HO scale layout to look like ordinary spike heads, as shown in the illustration. These spike-head feeders are only a little larger than the heads of the track spikes, and when painted to match the rails, the feeders practically disappear.

Solder wire and track feeders

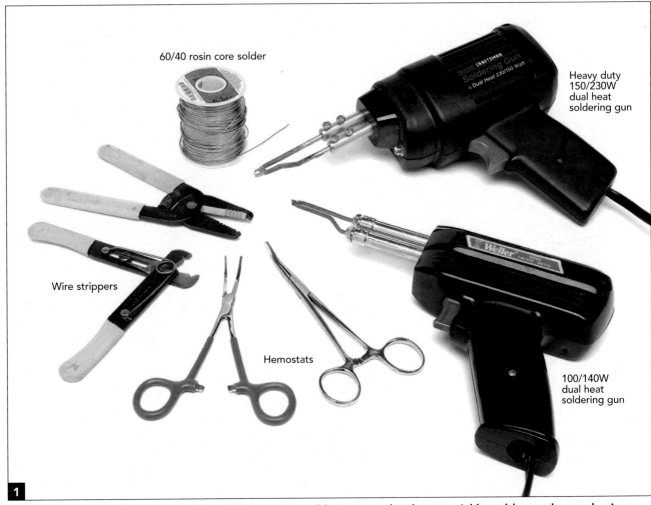

60/40 rosin core solder

Heavy duty 150/230W dual heat soldering gun

Wire strippers

Hemostats

100/140W dual heat soldering gun

1

All you need to produce good soldered joints are a soldering gun that heats quickly, solder, and some basic tools. Hemostats can be used as heat sinks to control the heat transfer.

Soldering has been used to secure electrical connections to the rails and control devices since the model railroad hobby began. It's a good skill to have, as soldered connections are handy in many situations. There's nothing difficult about the process, but there are some things you need to know for the best results.

A soldering gun that heats quickly is the handiest tool for most model railroad purposes, **1**. The 140 watt (W) size will handle most jobs, but veteran modelers prefer a dual-heat gun that toggles between 100 and 140W outputs as you pull or partially release the trigger. The lower heat range is handy for electronic work where you don't want to overheat the components.

Many types of solder are available, but the one to use for model railroad wiring is 60/40 (60 percent tin and 40 percent lead) solder with a rosin core. I prefer the small-diameter solder that's sold for electronic work because you can more easily control the amount applied.

Never use acid flux to solder any electrical component because the residue causes internal corrosion over time. This warning also applies to the so-called noncorrosive fluxes. I never use any flux for electrical work, including track wiring, that isn't a rosin product.

A wire stripper makes it easier to remove the insulation from wire. Wire strippers come in a variety of sizes, but most modelers find that an economy version does fine. Just make sure the tool is adjusted to avoid nicking the conductor, or the wire may break when it's bent.

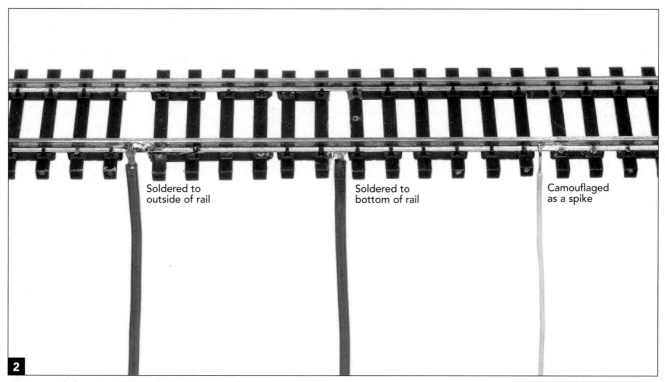

Soldered to
outside of rail

Soldered to
bottom of rail

Camouflaged
as a spike

2

Most modelers install track feeders on the outside of rails, but inside is okay too using a no. 22 AWG wire that's neatly soldered along the inside base of the rail. Track feeders can also be concealed underneath or camouflaged as a spike.

Both solid and stranded copper wire is available in numerical sizes. The heaviest wire has the lowest number. Wire diameter gets progressively smaller as the numbers go up. Heavy wire (nos. 12 or 14) is commonly used for the bus wires on layouts with Digital Command Control, while most other wiring can be done with intermediate sizes (16 or 18). Solid wire is easier to use in control panels and for feeders that are soldered to the rails. However, stranded wire is more flexible for applications where movement is desirable, such as a tethered cab or a control panel in a drawer.

Heat-activated bonding

Soldering is a heat-activated chemical bonding process, and the metals involved must be clean. Stripping off the insulation usually exposes a clean copper-wire end to work with, but wire salvaged from a previous layout may need to be cleaned with fine sandpaper.

A strong mechanical joint ensures a good soldered connection, so I always hook the wire end into the opening in a terminal on electrical switches or in

a terminal strip. If the connection is a splice, I make sure both wire ends are properly wrapped around each other.

Use the soldering gun to heat one side of the joint and then touch the solder to the opposite side of the wires. When the joint is hot enough, the solder melts and flows freely into the joint. Remove the heat and allow the joint to cool undisturbed for a few seconds. A good soldered joint will have a bright smooth surface that follows the wire shapes.

Soldering track feeders

Soldering feeders to the rails is a bit more difficult, as you need to control the heat to avoid melting the plastic ties. For a normal connection, I begin by cleaning the side of the rail with a needle file. Then I position the feeder wire, push the plastic ties back (when using flextrack), and clamp hemostats on the rail on both sides of the connection to serve as heat sinks, **2**. Wet tissue paper packed on the ties also helps protect ties from the heat. Then I heat the soldering gun so it's hot before I touch the tip to the railhead and apply the solder. As soon as the solder flows

into the joint, I remove the hot tip and let the joint cool.

Some modelers prefer to hide feeders. They wire the track sections before installation by soldering short lengths of wire to the underside of the rails. As the track is installed, they drill holes to drop these short feeders through the roadbed where they're connected to a terminal strip or the layout bus wires.

A neat trick that Andy Sperandeo uses is to strip the feeder wire and bring it up through a close-fitting hole in a wood tie (see page 25). He puts a right-angle bend in the end of the wire and flattens it slightly to make the soldered connection look like a spike. Once the rail is painted, the connection blends right in.

If you still have any misgivings about soldering, it's easy enough to practice with a few scraps of wire and a few track sections. Start by making a couple of wire splices and then move on to track feeders. Don't worry if you melt a few plastic ties because they're easily replaced with stripwood. Learning how to solder isn't difficult, and with a little practice, you'll soon be doing a perfect job.

STRUCTURES

Although trains are the stars of the show, structures have an important place on our model railroads. Today, manufacturers offer structures in a variety of media, and I'll show you how to work with plastic and wood kits.

If you can't find a structure kit that matches your favorite prototype, that's okay. Scratchbuilding and kitbashing (combining parts from two or more kits)

are popular pastimes for many modelers. I've included examples of how I scratchbuilt a depot from styrene following prototype plans and another on how I kitbashed a low-relief power plant from commercial kits.

Whether built from a kit, scratchbuilt, or kitbashed, structures can help give your layout a sense of place. Though most of the examples shown here are in HO scale, these techniques can be adapted for other scales.

Scratchbuild a station from drawings

Like many modelers, I enjoy studying prototype drawings. Whether it's a locomotive, freight car, or structure, it's fun to examine a drawing and think about what it would take to model the subject. But for *Model Railroader*'s Virginian Ry. project layout, I had to quit dreaming and turn plans into reality—in this case, the HO scale Reid Gap depot, **1**.

Though the depot is located in the fictional town of Reid Gap, I modeled it after the full-size building at Cullen, Va. If modeling accurate structures is your goal, try scratchbuilding from prototype drawings.

Scratchbuilding may seem intimidating, but it isn't. Start with a small project and you'll gain confidence. I've flubbed some projects over the years, but I learned from those experiences. The key to getting better is to keep building.

It's also important to work in a medium that you're comfortable with. Wood, styrene, and brass are some popular options. For this project, I used styrene, but I could just as easily have used wood board-and-batten siding for the walls.

Prototype drawings can be found in a variety of places. *Model Railroader* and other hobby magazines regularly publish drawings. Most railroad historical societies have collections of locomotive, freight car, and structure diagrams. And don't overlook city, county, and state museums. They may have the drawings you need to take your next project from a dream to reality. And wouldn't you know it, not long after I built this depot, American Model Builders released a kit for it!

Prototype drawings
Plans for the Cullen, Va., depot were published in *The Virginian Railway*

1 The scratchbuilt Reid Gap depot was based on drawings of a depot in Cullen, Va., which included an agent's office, a freight room with loading dock, and an open passenger waiting area.

Handbook (H-W Publications, 1985, out of print), **2**. Though not specified, the drawings are S scale. To convert them to HO scale, I photocopied them at 73.5 percent. (Reduce 40 percent for N scale and enlarge 133.3 percent for O scale.) The depot's footprint is 13'-4" x 30'-4". The dock measures 8'-0" x 12'-2" and is 3'-6" tall.

I was fortunate that the book also included photos of all four sides of the depot, as well as a close-up of the passenger shelter. The latter was helpful for accurately re-creating the bracing.

Depot and shelter
I prefer working with styrene for scratchbuilding, so I used Evergreen no. 4543 board-and-batten siding for the walls. However, for the windows to seat flush, I had to carefully trim away the battens around each opening, **3**.

With the door and window openings cut, I assembled the walls. To

prevent the walls from bowing, I added interior bracing. I used the thicker styrene strips because the depot model is for our 4 x 8 Virginian project railroad. The layout is transported to local train shows and subject to extreme temperature swings. The .100" x .100" strip would be sufficient throughout if the depot is on a permanent home layout, **4**.

I built the passenger shelter as a separate piece using the same board-and-batten styrene for the walls. Then I added the interior bracing using scale 2 x 4 and 4 x 4 styrene strip, **5**.

Windows and roof
I used stock Tichy Train Group windows for all but the rear freight room window. For that, I cut a Tichy six-light window (no. 8023) in half, **6**. To do so, I removed the upper two muntins with a sprue cutter. Then I used a razor saw and miter box to cut the sash. I used a jeweler's file to smooth the sash before

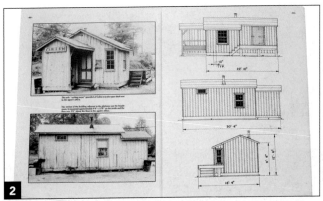

2 Scaled prototype drawings and photos showing all four sides of the depot made scratchbuilding easy to do.

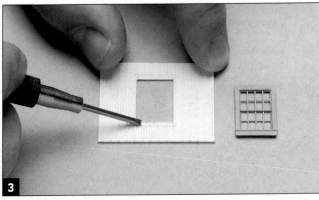

3 Using a chisel, I carefully trimmed the battens from the window openings, so they would fit flush.

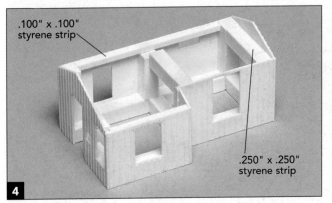

.100" x .100" styrene strip

.250" x .250" styrene strip

4 Although I used thicker styrene, .100" x .100" strip works well for buildings used on home layouts.

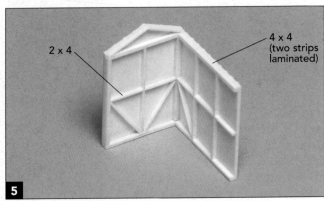

2 x 4

4 x 4 (two strips laminated)

5 I added interior bracing to the passenger shelter walls using scale 2 x 4 and 4 x 4 styrene strip.

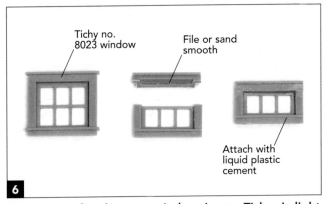

Tichy no. 8023 window

File or sand smooth

Attach with liquid plastic cement

6 For the rear freight room window, I cut a Tichy six-light window in half.

7 I used a Microbrush to paint the back of the windows black, so viewers cannot see through the structure.

attaching the two pieces with liquid plastic cement.

I painted all of the windows and trim Polly Scale Oxide Red with an airbrush. After the paint dried, I applied Woodland Scenics Scenic Accent Glue to the backs of the muntins. Once the glue turned clear, I applied .010" clear styrene window glazing.

Since the depot is near the front edge of the layout, the lack of an interior would be quite obvious. To prevent viewers from seeing through the structure, I painted the back of the clear styrene windows Polly Scale Steam Power Black, **7**.

I made the roof from .040" plain styrene sheet. To simulate the tar paper roofing, I cut printer paper into 5⁄16" strips. Then I sprayed the roof and the back of the paper with 3M Super 77 adhesive. I applied the strips from bottom to top, with a 1⁄16" overlap between rows, **8**.

I brush-painted the roof Polly Scale Tarnished Black. To give the roof a weathered and slightly faded appearance, I drybrushed it with L&N Gray, **9**. I then sprayed the bottom of the roof Light Undercoat Gray to match the walls. Next, I brush-painted the trim Oxide Red, being careful to keep the color off the roof. I also drilled a hole in the roof for the JL Innovative Design chimney, which I added later.

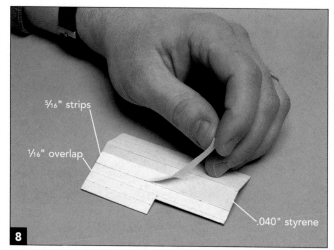

8 5/16" strips
1/16" overlap
.040" styrene

I sprayed strips of printer paper with adhesive and placed them bottom to top on the styrene-sheet roof.

9

First, I brush-painted the roof black and then drybrushed with gray to give it a weathered look.

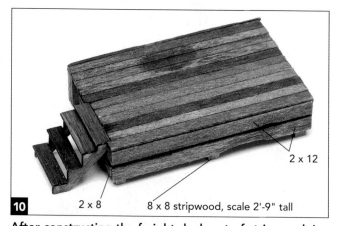

10 2 x 8   8 x 8 stripwood, scale 2'-9" tall   2 x 12

After constructing the freight dock out of stripwood, I stained it with an India ink wash and let it dry overnight.

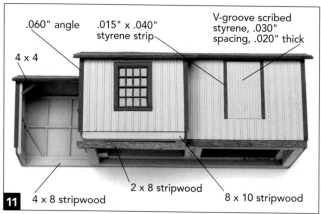

11
.060" angle   .015" x .040" styrene strip   V-groove scribed styrene, .030" spacing, .020" thick
4 x 4
4 x 8 stripwood   2 x 8 stripwood   8 x 10 stripwood

I inset the wood slightly so the stained stripwood, would be flush with the board part of the siding.

Freight dock

I switched gears and used stripwood for the freight dock. First, I stained all the wood with an India ink wash (2 teaspoons ink to 1 pint 70 percent isopropyl alcohol) and let it dry overnight, **10**.

Next, I cut the dock's sub-platform from .060" black styrene sheet. I cut notches in the styrene for the 8 x 8 stripwood legs. Each leg is a scale 2'-9" tall.

After the stain dried, I used cyanoacrylate adhesive (CA) to attach the legs and 2 x 8s to the styrene. I also used CA to cement the 2 x 12s to the legs. I didn't attach 2 x 12s to the side of the dock against the building. I used Quick Steps from Bar Mills for the short staircase.

Painting and final details

Before painting the depot, I attached 4 x 8 (passenger shelter) and 8 x 10

(depot and freight office) stripwood to the base of the depot with CA. I inset the wood slightly so the stained 2 x 8 stripwood, which I added after the depot was painted, would be flush with the board part of the board-and-batten siding, **11**.

I airbrushed the depot and trim Polly Scale Light Undercoat Gray. Then I painted the trim with the same firm's Oxide Red.

I used styrene for the two station signs. Each sign is .020" x .125" strip, and the trim is .015" x .030" strip. The sign's size will vary depending on the station name.

Since I didn't feel like firing up the airbrush for two small parts, I spray painted the signs white and brush-painted the trim Polly Scale Steam Power Black. After the paint dried, I applied a clear gloss coat before adding Microscale block

gothic lettering. I sprayed the signs with a clear flat finish and set them aside.

Weathering

When comparing the model to a color prototype photo of the Cullen depot in the *Virginian Railway in Color* (Morning Sun Books, 2005), my depot looked far too clean. To suggest that the building had been around a few years, I weathered it with a dusting of thinned Polly Scale Dirt (one part paint, four parts 70 percent isopropyl alcohol). I kept the airbrush parallel to the battens, and applied the paint heaviest at the base and feathered it out as I worked up.

With the weathering applied, I installed the final details, including a bench for the passenger shelter, a 4 x 4 stripwood step for the agent's office door, and the two station signs.

Make simple hoses

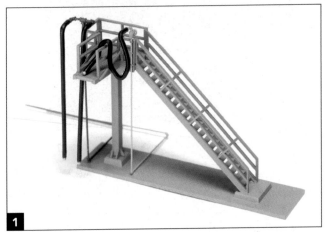

1 I used the casing from 22 gauge wire to model hoses for the tank car riser at an LP gas plant. The valves, tees, unions, and elbows were designed for steam locomotive models.

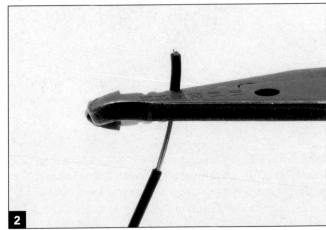

2 Use a pair of wire strippers to remove a short piece of casing on the 22 gauge wire.

3 With the wire exposed, gently pull it out of the casing with needlenose pliers.

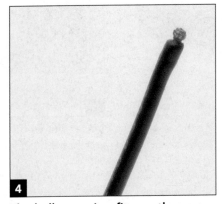

4 The hollow casing fits neatly over the nubs on the brass unions.

5 Bead and jewelry cord is another option for modeling hoses. It's found at craft stores and comes in various gauges.

One of the industries on *Model Railroader*'s HO scale Milwaukee, Racine & Troy club layout is an LP gas plant. I modified a tank car riser from a Walthers North American Ethanol series kit (no. 933-2980), and I used valves, tees, unions, and elbows from Precision Scale and Custom Finishing to model the pipes and controls, **1**. However, I struggled finding a solution for realistic hoses. Then it dawned on me to use 22 gauge wire casing.

I started by clipping a piece of casing off the wire with a pair of wire strippers, **2**. With the wire exposed, I used a pair of needlenose pliers to gently remove it, leaving me with a hollow casing, **3**. The brass unions that I used had small nubs on the ends, and that worked to my advantage because I could slip the casing right over the top, **4**. If you need the hose to maintain its shape, use 22 gauge solid wire.

Another option is to use different types of bead and jewelry cord, **5**. As with wire, it comes in various gauges. Since there is no wire inside, you can cut it with scissors or a single-edge razor blade.

Although I made hoses for an LP plant, you could easily adapt this technique for hoses on a locomotive sanding tower and other locations where hoses are used.

CODY SAYS:

If you don't want to buy an entire kit to get one part, GLX Scale Models (glxscalemodels.com) sells a two-pack of tank car risers. The kit includes wire for the hoses and pipes.

Model a weather-beaten structure

1

This Northern Pacific class C depot has seen better days as it has been modeled as a weather-beaten wood structure, complete with peeling paint, broken windows, and a damaged roof.

In model railroading, weathering is typically associated with freight cars and locomotives. However, weathering structures is another way to add realism to your layout, **1**. Peeling and faded paint, a roof in need of repair, and broken glass are just a few of the ways to turn an ordinary structure into a standout weather-beaten model.

For this modeling project, I used an American Model Builders HO scale Northern Pacific class C depot kit. Though I've built structures in plastic, brass, and plaster, I prefer wood for detailed weathering projects like this.

Structure weathering doesn't have to be limited to just the walls. On many layouts, the roof is the most visible part of a building. Vents, air conditioners, and antennas, among other things, can make the roof visually interesting. Although I didn't need those details here, I enhanced the depot roof by leaving shingles off this abandoned structure, exposing the bare subroof. I also painted individual shingles to look

like patchwork repairs had been made over the years.

You'll be surprised by how easy it is to turn an ordinary wood kit into one that will get the attention of visitors and members of your operating crew. Give these techniques a try. You'll like the results.

Stains
It's easy to give wood that gray, aged look with stains. Timberline Scenery, Micro-Mark, and Hunterline, among others, offer factory-mixed stains in a variety of colors, **2**. You can use the stains individually or in combination to create different effects.

Another option is to mix your own stains with India ink (available at most art supply and craft stores) or acrylic paint and 70 percent isopropyl alcohol. My favorite mix is 2 teaspoons of India ink to 1 pint of isopropyl alcohol. You can make the stain lighter or darker

by adjusting the amount of ink. For a warm-tone stain, substitute sepia ink for India ink.

Applying the stain
I stained the walls of the NP depot with the India ink wash. I applied the wash with a ½" paintbrush, brushing with the wood grain, **3**. I used all of the stain on the brush before reloading it. This technique yields a variety of light, medium, and dark gray planks.

Since 70 percent isopropyl alcohol contains 30 percent water, the India ink wash may warp the wood parts. To prevent this, I laid the wet parts on a flat surface, covered them with paper towels, and laid heavy books on top of them. I let the stain dry for 48 hours.

Bracing
The depot walls have a milled siding pattern that's flexible across the grain.

2 Using stains is an easy way to give wood an aged appearance. You can use one stain or combine them to produce different effects.

3 Wood takes stain differently. The basswood wall in the background required only one application, while I had to apply two coats of stain to the microplywood roof brackets.

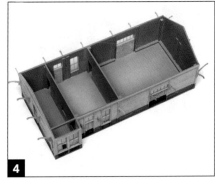

4 Using pieces of stripwood, I braced the walls to prevent them from warping or sagging. I then primed the interior walls and painted them green.

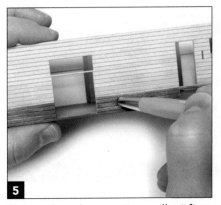

5 To weather the exterior walls, I first scraped off the paint with a Micro-Mark's Distresser weathering brush to expose the stained wood.

6 After removing the fuzz left by the Distresser brush with a 3M wood-finishing pad, I used the pad to weather the walls by removing the sand and brown paint.

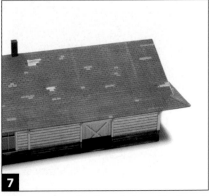

7 I began weathering the roof when I added the peel-and-stick, three-tab shingles. I left some areas bare to expose the subroof.

To prevent the walls from warping or sagging over time, I braced them from the inside using assorted pieces of stripwood, **4**. Then I masked the exterior walls and sprayed the interior with Rust-Oleum Gray Automobile Primer. Once the primer dried, I painted the interior walls with Model Master Pale Green.

Distresser and finishing pad weathering

Next, I masked the interior and sprayed the exterior with Polly Scale Sand and NP Dark Brown (three parts Roof Brown, one part Boxcar Red).

I let the paint dry for 24 hours and then used Micro-Mark's Distresser weathering brush to scrape off the paint and expose the stained wood, **5**. Having the bristles exposed about ³⁄₁₆"

is ideal for heavy weathering. If you prefer a lighter touch, expose more of the bristles.

I used a 3M wood-finishing pad (no. 07415) to remove fuzz created by the Distresser brush. In the process, I discovered that the pad works well for weathering too. I used it to lightly remove the sand and brown paint, **6**. I also used the pad to weather the delicate peel-and-stick cardstock trim. Before weathering the building, I applied blue painter's tape where the station sign would have been.

After I finished using the Distresser brush and wood-finishing pad, I applied a final wash of India ink. This stained any bare wood exposed by the Distresser brush and further muted the paint. Once the wash dried, I attached the trim. Don't apply an alcohol-based wash after the

peel-and-stick trim has been attached to the model, as this may cause the adhesive to come off.

Roof weathering

I weathered the roof fairly heavily to reinforce the abandoned nature of the depot. I started by applying the peel-and-stick, three-tab shingles, omitting random patches to reveal the bare subroof, **7**.

Next, I brush-painted the shingles Polly Scale Union Pacific Dark Gray. I highlighted individual shingles by painting them with the same firm's Roof Brown and Louisville & Nashville Gray.

I then used a Microbrush to apply Hunterline Light Gray wood stain to the subroof. I applied the alcohol-based stained sparingly, so it wouldn't attack the shingles' adhesive backing.

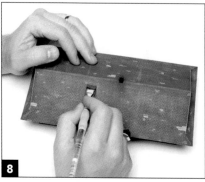

8
After painting the shingles and staining the bare spots of the subroof, I drybrushed the shingles, which highlighted raised edges and details.

9
To add to the abandoned look of the station, I broke some glass (actually, clear styrene) in the operator's bay.

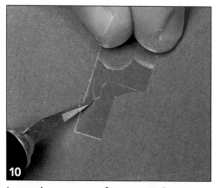

10
I cut the panes of one window out of the styrene, leaving all but a corner missing from the lower right pane.

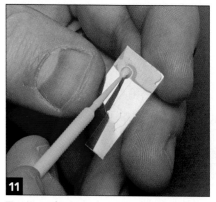

11
To give the windows a dirty, grimy look, I brushed on some Polly Scale Clear Flat.

12
You can create a peeling-paint effect on a building by using rubber cement masks, as I did on this shed. Apply the rubber cement randomly and then paint the building.

13
After the paint dries, use a no. 11 blade to remove the masks. The masks can be hard to see, so you might want to mark their location on a sketch of the building.

I highlighted the shingles by drybrushing them with L&N Gray, **8**. I dipped the brush into the paint, wiped off all but a trace amount on a paper towel, and lightly dragged the brush over the shingles. The idea is to highlight raised edges and details.

I finished weathering the roof by adding soot stains to the chimney and nearby shingles with an airbrush.

Broken glass

I modeled the broken glass in the operator's bay using the kit's clear styrene, **9**. First, I marked the locations of the four panes. Next, I cut all but a corner out of the lower right pane, **10**. I simulated the shatter marks with a no. 11 blade.

To suggest that the windows are dirty, I used a Microbrush to apply Polly Scale Clear Flat on the opposite side of the styrene from the scribe

marks, **11**. I prefer the Clear Flat over aerosol Testor's Dullcote as the latter gives the clear glazing a frosted look. My goal was to simulate dirt and grime while keeping the windows somewhat transparent.

Peeling paint

It's easy to simulate peeling paint on buildings with rubber cement masks. Using a no. 0 brush, I applied rubber cement randomly along the wood grain on a motor car shed kit from the Northern Pacific Ry. Historical Association (nprha.org), **12**. I masked individual boards instead of large areas.

Rubber cement masks can be hard to see once the building is painted. It's a good idea to mark where you applied the masks on the kit's instructions or on a sketch of the building.

I painted the shed with the same colors I used on the depot. Once the paint dried, I used a no. 11 blade to remove the masks, **13**.

You can also remove the rubber cement masks with tape or an art gum eraser. If you use an art gum eraser, you can rub it over the entire wall and not have to remember where the rubber cement is.

CODY SAYS:

You can further enhance the abandoned look of the depot by adding random junk piles outside of the building or surrounding the structure with chain link fence.

Put a big industry in a small space

1

A coal-fired power plant is one of the first things you see when viewing the HO scale Milwaukee, Racine & Troy.

Whether you're on a date, at a business meeting, or hosting a model railroad open house, you always want to make a good first impression. Though we have many beautifully finished scenes on the *Model Railroader*'s HO scale Milwaukee, Racine & Troy club layout, the first things visitors see when they enter the room is a big blue backdrop, plywood benchwork, and unballasted track. To give the entrance to our model railroad some visual interest, I added a low-relief coal-fired power plant.

Modeling the Wisconsin Electric power plant was more than building Walthers Tri-State Power Authority (kit no. 933-3055) and plunking it on the layout. The kit's footprint is 10" x 13⅞", which would cover a siding and the MR&T's double-track main line. A better option was to turn the three-dimensional kit into a low-relief structure and expand it horizontally by kitbashing two kits to better fill the 9" x 38" space I had to work with, **1**.

In addition to the Walthers kits, I used Pikestuff's Shop kit, no. 15, to represent an enclosed shed for the rotary dumper. I trimmed 4" off the building, but it still looks realistic.

Do you need a lot of space for a big industry? Not always. By converting full kits to low-relief structures, you can add a power plant, steel mill, or whatever industry you want in a relatively small space.

Paper mock-up
Before I took a no. 11 blade to a pair of $65 kits, I made a paper mock-up to verify that my plan would work, **2**. It's easier to modify a paper structure than to rework a plastic kit.

I started by photocopying the kit parts that I planned to use. Some of the end walls were too large to copy on a single 11 x 17 sheet, so I made the first copy, repositioned the panels, and made the second copy. I cut out the copied parts, taped them to cardboard, and

placed the mock-up on the layout. I marked the opening on the right end of the plant where trains pass through the building to reach hidden storage tracks.

Scoring and snapping
I needed to reduce the side walls (nos. 102 and 105) to 6⅛" wide. To do this, I scored the panels with a no. 11 blade and snapped the plastic apart. I started by placing the blade against the edge of the corrugation at the top of the wall and carefully dragging it the length of the wall. Work slowly here, especially with the first few passes, as it's easy for the knife to wander off course and damage the molded detail.

After making a half dozen passes with the front of the blade, I flipped it over and used the back edge to speed up the scoring process, **3**. Using the back of the blade removes more material on each pass.

I made six more passes with the back of the blade before snapping the

2 To test the fit of my power plant, I made a paper mock-up and placed it on the layout.

3 Using the back edge of the blade helps speed up the scoring process.

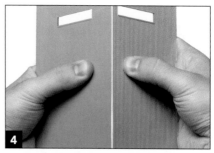

4 Carefully flex the wall back and forth along the scored line until it snaps apart.

5 Gaps in the wall joints can be filled with styrene rod and liquid plastic cement appled with a Microbrush.

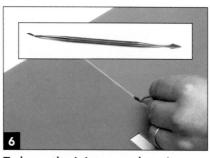

6 To keep the joints seamless, I shaved away the excess styrene with a stainless steel carving tool.

7 Use an abrasive pad to finish blending the seam. The pads conform well to the metal siding.

wall. I carefully flexed the wall back and forth along the line I'd scored until it snapped apart, **4**. Don't apply a lot of pressure when snapping the plastic, as this may damage the walls. Once the wall panels were separated, I cleaned up the edges with a mill file so the walls would seat flush against the backdrop.

Splicing wall panels

I doubled the length of the front walls by splicing together two wall panels on the upper and lower levels (parts 104 and 103, respectively). Straight from the box, these walls have beveled edges on the left and right to meet with the side walls. However, to form a flush butt joint on the wider plant, I squared off the edges where the panels meet in the middle.

Though I was careful when I cut and filed the plastic wall panels, there were still gaps. I filled the gaps with .010" styrene rod and liquid plastic cement. First, I set the styrene rod in the gap. Then I applied the cement with a Microbrush, **5**. As the styrene started to soften, I pressed it into the gap.

I let the glue dry for 24 hours before smoothing the joint with a double-ended stainless steel carving tool (the kind used for wax and ceramics). I carefully shaved away the excess styrene rod to form a seamless joint. Then I made several light passes with the carving tool, being careful not to gouge the plastic, **6**.

I finished blending the seam with a product not typically associated with model railroading, a Scotch-Brite no. 7448 abrasive hand pad (available at most auto part stores and building supply centers). In the past, I had used sandpaper for tasks like this, but it didn't conform well to the siding.

Then I remembered the abrasive pads my dad used at his auto body repair shop for prepping plastic bumpers. I tried the pad here and it worked great. The pad conformed well to the contours of the corrugated metal siding, and it also removed the plastic fuzz left over from the carving tool, **7**.

Plugging openings

With two kits, there are plenty of extra wall sections to cut up to fill unwanted door and window openings. For example, when I spliced the two no. 104 wall panels, there were two door openings. To disguise the fact that I spliced two of the same parts, I filled the door on the right with a scrap piece of wall panel, **8**. I cut the plastic slightly oversize, and then used a file and sanding sticks to remove enough material for it to fit in the opening. I set the plug into the wall with liquid plastic cement. Then I brushed two coats of cement along the joint, which helped fill the seam. I smoothed the seam with the abrasive hand pad I used earlier.

Bracing

The key to success when building big structures is sufficient bracing. Over time, plastic walls may bow or door openings curl. To prevent this, I braced the butt joints with .040" styrene sheet and the walls and roof with .250" x .250" styrene strip, **9**.

For those of you now in the digital photography age, you can put those no-longer-needed plastic slide mounts to use as corner braces for structures, **10**. I like using plastic slide mounts for the corners, but cardboard mounts will also work. If you use the latter, you'll need to cement them to the building with cyanoacrylate adhesive. If you don't have a stock of slide mounts, triangles cut from styrene will work just as well.

Where I spliced two identical wall panels, I filled one door with a scrap piece of wall panel.

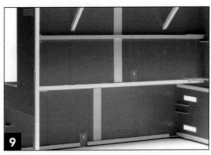

Plastic walls in big buildings may bow, so I braced the butt joints, walls, and roof with styrene.

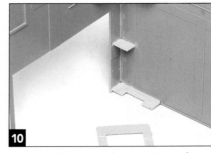

For sturdy corner braces, I used plastic slide mounts. You can also use triangles cut from styrene.

The model needed rooftop details, so I added exhaust stacks, vents, and an air conditioner unit.

I built a structure to house the plant's rotary dumper from a Pikestuff's Shop kit.

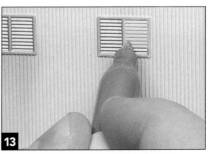

To avoid masking and airbrushing, I simply used a silver paint marker to color the vents.

Rooftop details

I replaced the stock roof with .040" styrene sheet and attached it with liquid plastic cement. When I stood back and surveyed the building, it was too plain. To see how full-size, coal-fired power plants looked, I used Google Earth. Satellite images of plants in southeastern Wisconsin revealed that my model was lacking rooftop details. Blowers, vents, and air conditioners were just some of the things I could add to enhance the buildings.

Fortunately, I had a pack of roof details (no. 933-3733) from Walthers. The set includes more than 30 parts, of which I used four short T-style exhaust stacks, three tall monitor vents with round bases, and a medium rooftop air conditioner, **11**.

Although the details are shown on the unpainted building, I didn't glue them on until I painted the structure. I spray-painted the rooftop details with Floquil Bright Silver. I let the paint dry for 24 hours, and I then toned down the silver with Model Master Lusterless Flat (Testor's Dullcote would also work). I lightly weathered the rooftop details with thinned Polly Scale Steam Power Black.

Rotary dump shed

Most modern power plants have a covered building that houses a rotary dumper, and I made one using Pikestuff's Shop kit, **12**. I built most of the kit following the instructions, while leaving off the office and the wall that would be against the backdrop (which I made from .040" styrene sheet). The door opening is 3¹⁄₁₆" x 4³⁄₁₆". In addition to the supplied roof vents, I added motorized vents and a motorized blower from the Walthers vent set.

Painting and weathering

Even though the Walthers and Pikestuff buildings have different siding, I was able to give the structures a unified corporate look with paint. I started by spraying both structures with Rust-Oleum Gray Automobile Primer.

Then I airbrushed the buildings. I used Polly Scale Sand on the siding, Roof Brown on the bag house and rotary dump shed roofs and on the power plant trim, Union Pacific Dark Gray on the power plant roof and bag house legs, and Concrete on the stack and building foundations.

I weathered the buildings with thinned L&N Gray and Steam Power

Black (one part paint to four parts 70 percent isopropyl alcohol). I built up the weathering in thin layers, as it's easier to add more weathering than it is to remove it.

Though corrugated siding is appropriate for the power plant, it's a pain to mask over. Instead of masking the bag house and then airbrushing its vents, I used a silver paint marker to color in these details, **13**. Then, I applied an India ink wash to the vents (2 teaspoons India ink to 1 pint 70 percent isopropyl alcohol).

Finishing touches

By doubling the length of the front walls of the power plant, I was able to fill the 9" x 38" space. I then just needed to add a few finishing touches.

Scenicking around the power plant was easy. I used N scale limestone ballast, with some HO scale cinders sprinkled in, for the driveways. Then I installed BLMA chain link fence around the plant's perimeter. Though two tracks go into the rotary-dump shed, I added a siding long enough for one car, so we could spot a flatcar loaded with heavy equipment for the plant.

Glaze windows with adhesive

1 Microscale Kristal Klear works well for glazing windows on smaller structures. You can also use Testor's Clear Parts Cement & Window Maker.

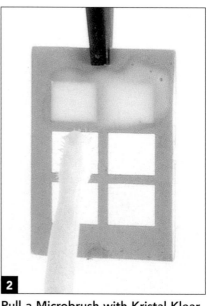

2 Pull a Microbrush with Kristal Klear across the window pane. Work from the back of the window to keep the material off the window frame.

Microscale Kristal Klear is a versatile adhesive that, not only can be used to secure clear parts to models, can be used as window glazing, **1**. I also used it to make taillights and turn signals, as described on page 85. It only takes a few simple steps to turn the adhesive into window glazing. Kristal Klear works best on smaller window panes.

Start by dipping a Microbrush into the Kristal Klear. Then, working from the back of the window, set the brush into the corner of the pane and drag it across, **2**. The Kristal Klear comes out of the bottle white, but it dries clear. Repeat this process until all of the panes are filled. It takes about 45 minutes for the Kristal Klear to dry.

Though I used this technique on structure windows, **3**, it also works well for door glazing, vehicle windows, and smaller windows on cabooses, locomotives, and passenger cars.

3 The windows on this HO scale Northern Pacific shed were finished with Kristal Klear. It takes about 45 minutes for the windows to dry to a clear finish.

Cast your own wall sections

1 This freight house was made from modular wall sections and wall sections cast from resin.

2 For the master wall section, I modified a blank wall section.

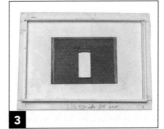

3 As a form for the mold, I cemented the master wall in a shallow styrene box.

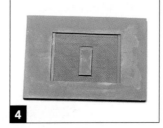

4 After the rubber hardened, I removed the mold from the box.

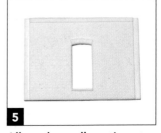

5 Allow the wall sections to harden, and they're ready for use in your structures.

On *Model Railroader*'s Beer Line project railroad, the majority of the layout's structures were either kit-bashed or scratchbuilt. The Milwaukee Road freight house was a long, narrow, two-story brick building. I built the freight house using Design Preservation Models (DPM) modular wall sections for the first floor and wall castings I made for the second floor, **1**.

Here's how I made the wall sections DPM didn't offer. I made a master from a couple of extra DPM wall sections and then made a silicone rubber mold to cast the single-window wall sections with two-part resin. The mold and casting materials are from Micro-Mark's no. 82698 casting starter set.

To make the master wall section, I started with a blank wall, **2**. After carefully cutting a new window opening, I added a brick lintel and sill that I shaved off an extra window section. I cemented the assembled master wall to the bottom of a shallow styrene box that I made as a form for the mold, **3**.

I mixed a batch of room-temperature-vulcanizing (RTV) silicone rubber and poured it into the mold box. I removed the finished mold from the box after the RTV rubber hardened, **4**. Making several identical molds speeds the production of finished parts.

The two-part casting resin has a working life of 3 minutes, and is ready to be de-molded after 15 minutes, although it takes longer to completely harden, **5**. I made a few more walls than I needed so I could discard any that had defects that might show on the model.

Once I'd gathered or cast all the wall sections I needed, I assembled them pretty much according to the DPM instructions.

Cut door and window openings

1 I used the Nibbler, a hand-operated cutting tool, to make door and window openings in the office for this LP plant. The Nibbler can be used on styrene up to 1⁄16" thick (or thinner sheet metal).

2 If a door goes to the bottom of a wall, mark the opening with a pencil and use the Nibbler to take bites out of the styrene.

3 If windows or doors are in the center, drill a hole in the middle of each opening to make room for the Nibbler's cutting head.

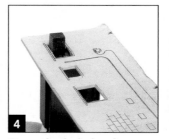

4 Once the hole has been drilled, use the Nibbler to cut away the rest of the styrene, but don't cut all the way to the pencil lines.

5 Use sanding sticks and jeweler's files to smooth the edges of the openings.

I enjoy scratchbuilding structures from styrene because it's easy to cut, it takes glue well, and it's readily available, **1**. Though cutting wall sections is easy, making door and window openings can be tedious. However, with the Nibbler cutting tool, you can cut openings quickly and accurately. The Nibbler is a hand-operated punch-and-die tool that cuts 3⁄32" bits out of styrene up to 1⁄16" thick

(or thinner sheet metal). It's available from Micro-Mark (micromark.com) and electronics supply houses.

For doors, I first outline the opening with a pencil. Then I use the Nibbler to cut away the styrene, **2**, test-fitting the door frequently to make sure I don't cut away too much material.

Windows and doors in the center of the styrene require a slightly different approach. Once I have the window

locations marked, I use a 15⁄64" bit to drill an opening in the center for the Nibbler's cutting head, **3**. Then I use the Nibbler to cut the styrene, **4**.

Don't cut all the way to the pencil lines for the openings. Instead, leave a bit of material and use sanding sticks and jeweler's files to finish, **5**.

If you plan on doing a lot of scratchbuilding with styrene, give the Nibbler a try. You'll be happy with the results.

Kitbash large modular structures

1

Photocopying actual kit parts and taping the cutouts onto cardboard to create full-size mock-ups of your buildings allows you to see how they fit on your layout.

Big buildings surround and usually tower above most city passenger stations, so I wanted to create a similar effect on *Model Railroader*'s HO club layout, the Milwaukee, Racine & Troy. In downtown Milwaukee, prototype trains literally run through "concrete canyons" as the tracks snake between rows of aging warehouses and vintage factories that line both sides of the main line.

Most of these buildings are older concrete and masonry structures that had numerous windows. However,

many of the windows that formerly provided plenty of natural light and ventilation are now covered.

Older buildings also include remnants of railroad service. Their track-level doorways may be bricked over now, but their shortened docks and platform footings are unmistakable details remaining from busier times.

Modeling big buildings takes some ingenuity and careful planning. Few layouts have room for a scale-size commercial warehouse, so modelers have to resort to some theatrical tricks and

build only what can be seen. In fact, all that's really needed is the wall or corner of the building facing the viewer.

However, I've found that printed background buildings are too flat and don't work well in our closeup environment. Thin walls or narrow structures with three-dimensional details look more realistic. Fortunately, modelers in HO and N scales have excellent modular building parts to work with, thanks to Design Preservation Models (DPM), Great West Models, and Walthers Cornerstone Modulars. It's also possible to open rectangular kits out into long flats for these situations (see page 36).

My red brick warehouse structure is made from DPM modular panels following the manufacturer's instructions. The modular pieces are interchangeable, so it's easy to include doorways, windows, and other details as desired.

Here's how I developed and built a brick seven-story warehouse for the MR&T.

Develop a plan

Planning templates are available from both DPM and Walthers, so I made multiple full-size photocopies of the parts I needed. If templates aren't available, you can photocopy the actual kit parts for your own planning purposes. Then I cut and carefully taped the copies together to determine the rough size of each wall. Finally, I taped the cutouts onto pieces of cardboard to create full-size mock-ups of my buildings.

Placing each mock-up on the layout allowed me to see exactly how it fit in, **1**. I also checked the doorway locations and made height adjustments. It's much easier to trim off some cardboard or rearrange the photocopied walls now than it will be to shorten or rework the plastic structure later on. Once I was happy with the fit, it was easy to count and order the modular parts I needed to build the structure.

Assemble each wall

I began assembly of the DPM components by trimming off the molding sprues and smoothing the edges of each panel with a file. I carefully looked for and removed any molding flash that interfered with seating the vertical pilaster trim between the modular wall panels during assembly.

I laid a carpenter's framing square on the bench to align the parts as I assembled each row of panels, **2**. Starting at one end with the top of the row upside-down and face up against the square, I made sure the parts were oriented properly (the top edge has a row of brick trim). Then I applied Tenax-7R liquid plastic cement, pressed the pilaster into place, and held each joint for a few seconds until the cement set.

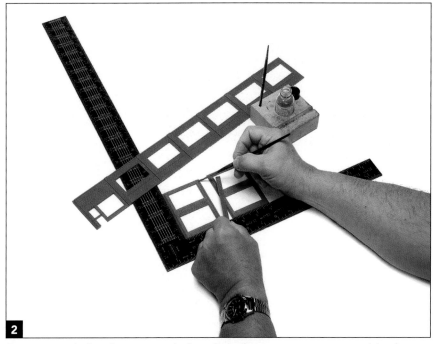

2 A carpenter's framing square helps align the parts as you assemble the rows of panels.

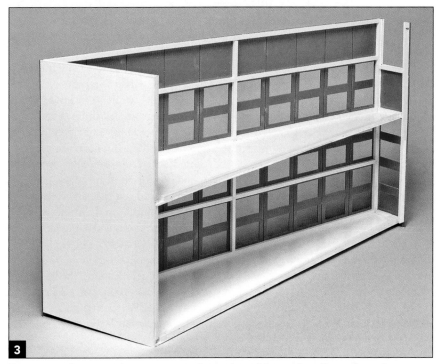

3 For areas that remain unseen, such as the wide end wall, roof, and intermediate floor, I used sheet styrene.

As soon as each joint had set, I applied cement to the next wall panel, slipped it under the pilaster, and again pressed the two into good contact.

I let these rows harden for an hour or so, then cleaned up the mating edges, and cemented together the horizontal rows.

Construct the building

Final assembly of the building began by cementing the front corner joint. I glued the top corner and held it tight until the cement set. Then I worked down the corner in small steps. Finally, I reinforced the corner joint with a vertical strip of ¼"-square styrene.

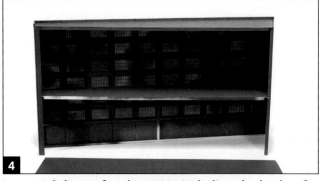

4 I sprayed the roof and interior, including the backs of the window glazing, black to hide the empty space.

5 I easily converted this Walthers American Hardware Supply kit into a flat to help fill a city skyline.

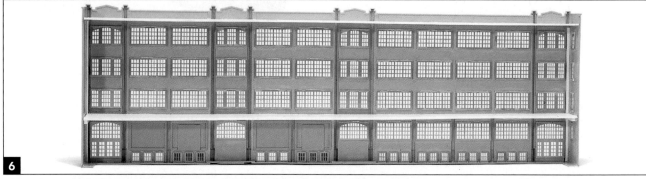

6 I lengthened the building using the kit's end walls and placed the doors and windows in different locations.

I used .080" sheet styrene for the wide end wall, roof, and intermediate floor, **3**. During assembly, I reinforced all of the edges and joints with pieces of ¼"-square styrene, being careful to avoid adding any bracing that interferes with the window frames.

The building's rear wall (not shown) is mounted with 2-56 round-head screws, driven into the ¼"-square bracing, to provide interior access later on, should it be needed.

I spray-painted the front walls Floquil Tuscan Red and then let the assembly dry.

Add windows

I left the window frames unpainted, but this is the time to paint them if you want a different color.

It's difficult to reach in and add window glazing inside a big building, so I cemented the clear styrene to the window frames before installation. I held each frame tight against the clear styrene and used a small paintbrush to carefully apply Tenax-7R around each frame. Then I let it set for a few minutes while I assembled several more windows. I used a pair of scissors to

trim the excess glazing even with the edges of the window frames.

The DPM windows fit inside the wall openings, so I positioned each frame in an opening and carefully applied Plastruct Bondene cement to secure it. I've found Bondene produces a good bond even if the edges of the opening have been painted. However, I was careful to keep the Bondene off the clear styrene and my fingers, as the cement will damage the plastic.

Finally, I sprayed the roof and inside of the building, including the backs of the window glazing, with Floquil Grimy Black, **4**. This step hides the empty interior but leaves the outside windows with reflections.

Flat conversion

Large building kits lend themselves to easy conversion into flats to help fill a city skyline. By rearranging the walls and moving details around, I turned a Walthers American Hardware Supply kit into a building less than 2" thick with a couple of loading docks, **5**.

The red walls are from a Walthers Backshop kit. By butting all four panels edge to edge, it was possible to get a

structure about 48" long. Using other combinations of parts from two kits made some different-looking flats. I finished them off with the kit's detail parts.

I used both end walls, separated by the original fancy front corners, to lengthen the structure, **6**. All of the doorways, docks, and windows came in the kit, but I used them in different locations. The end panels, set at right angles to the front wall, are the original kit's rear corners.

Finishing details

Further detailing is still needed to complete these downtown models, but many of the details depend on the final scene. Signs are a colorful and important feature on most older structures, and all sorts of them are available as decals and dry transfers. Some can be vintage signs from previous eras since few are ever removed. You can also add rooftop access stairways, elevator shafts, water tanks, air conditioning equipment, stacks, and vents. For inspiration, take a good look around you or study photos in books and magazines.

LOCOMOTIVES AND FREIGHT CARS

Today's locomotive and freight car models are some of the best the hobby's ever seen. Crisp molding, metal wheelsets, and road-number-specific details are just some of the features we've come to expect. However, just because a model is labeled ready to run doesn't mean it can't be enhanced.

Similar to vehicles, models require regular inspections and tune-ups. In this section, I've once again turned to

Jim Hediger to share his advice on keeping locomotives and freight cars running their best.

I'll follow up with an easy way to clean the wheels on your locomotives, model some details, and work with acetal handrails.

Making the stars of the show perform and look their best requires some effort. But in the end, you'll be rewarded with models that run reliably and look good

Perform rolling stock checkups

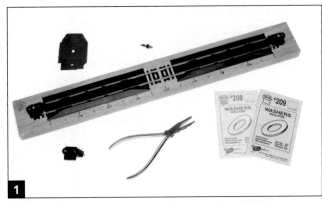

Useful tools for tuning up rolling stock include a coupler test fixture, truck tuner, NMRA Standards Gauge, height gauge, and a trip pin pliers.

This test fixture makes it easy to quickly check coupler height and make sure they align. It also helps check the position of uncoupling pins on freight cars.

Good rolling stock plays a major role in the operating quality of any layout. On most model railroads, the car fleet represents more potential problems than any other single element, so here's how I check every car before it goes on my Ohio Southern RR, using just a few handy tools, **1**.

Trucks and wheels

The majority of current HO cars come with RP-25 contour wheels, so I use an NMRA Standards Gauge to check every wheelset to make sure the wheels are in gauge and properly centered on the axle. After checking the gauge, I spin each axle and discard any with wheels that wobble or don't run true.

If a wheel adjustment is required, I grip the metal axle with a pair of needlenose pliers and use my fingers to twist the plastic wheels until they match the notches in the NMRA gauge.

I check new trucks for molding flash that may impede the car's free rolling qualities. Needle-point axles provide the best rolling qualities, but occasionally, I find a tight rigid-frame truck that squeezes the ends of the axles and effectively puts the brakes on. To resolve this problem, I use a double-ended jour-nal reaming tool called the HO Truck Tuner (Micro-Mark no. 82838).

Coupler test fixture

To speed up my freight car coupler inspections, I made a simple text fixture, **2**. I used a smooth piece of 1x3 as a base with a couple of Atlas no. 844 code 100 rerailers tacked along its center line. I mounted a Kadee coupler gauge at each end.

To use the fixture, I set a car in the middle and move it back and forth so the rerailers put the car on the track. Then I push the car from end to end to check coupler heights and uncoupling pin positions at both ends. If an adjust-ment is needed, Kadee and Micro-Mark sell special pliers for this job.

I use Kadee no. 208 (.015") and no. 209 (.010") fiber washers to make minor height adjustments until the car matches the height gauges. However, if more than a washer or two is required, I set the car aside for further work on the coupler boxes to avoid raising the model above its proper scale height.

Appropriate weight

My HO inspection fixture is marked in 1" increments, and then I calculated and added the appropriate NMRA RP-20.1 weight alongside the length marks. The recommended weight for an HO car is 1 ounce initial weight plus ½ ounce per inch of the car length.) When a car is coupled to a gauge, I can easily read what it should weigh when I put it on the scale.

I use a postal scale to weigh each car. If any adjustments are needed, I add stick-on weights or use double-faced pieces of foam mounting tape to add steel washers inside the car.

My last step is to adjust the truck kingpins—I tighten both trucks down until they're snug. Then I loosen one by half a turn, and the other by a full turn. This produces a steady-riding carbody, while the looser truck can still rock from side to side to pass over any small undulations in the track.

Maintaining the fleet

After my initial fleet inspections, I find that my cars seldom need much atten-tion. As I completed my car adjust-ments, the Ohio Southern's quality of operation steadily improved. Today, most of my derailments are caused by human error, so any car that derails on its own is immediately set aside for a full inspection before it returns to regular service.

Service locomotives

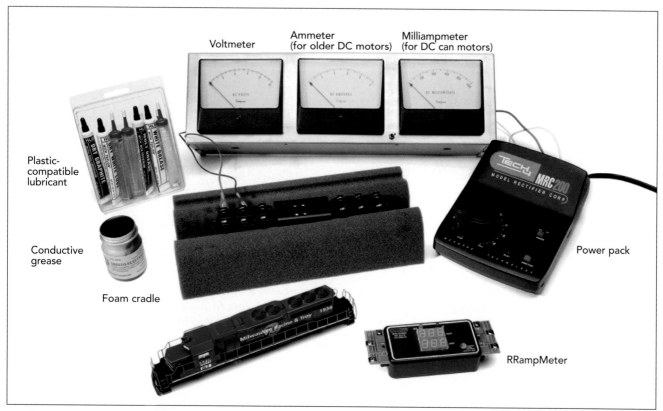

Voltmeter

Ammeter (for older DC motors)

Milliampmeter (for DC can motors)

Plastic-compatible lubricant

Conductive grease

Foam cradle

Power pack

RRampMeter

A metered power supply, locomotive cradle, test leads, and a few tools make it easy to clean and maintain HO locomotives for top performance.

Regular servicing and preventive maintenance play an important role in keeping any railroad operating reliably. I've developed an annual inspection that I perform on all of my regular operating locomotives. It's divided into three phases: testing, cleaning, and repairs.

Testing

To check a DC locomotive, I run it on a metered test track. My power pack includes a voltmeter and an ammeter, so I can see how well the mechanism performs. Older HO locomotives generally use about .3 amp of current, while newer can motors are more efficient, with readings around .1 amp. If a model draws a significantly higher current, I check for mechanical problems.

I also test my Digital Command Control (DCC) locomotives with a RRampMeter (sold by Tony's Train Exchange, tonystrains.com) to check the current. I also try the DCC functions to make sure they're working properly.

Cleaning

My second step is to remove the body shell and clean the mechanism. I use a ½" paintbrush to clean off accumulated dirt and lint. Then I invert the mechanism and set it in a cradle, connect test leads, and run it while I clean the wheel treads with a pipe cleaner dipped in track cleaner. Stubborn dirt deposits may need to be removed with an abrasive track cleaning block. I also check the electrical connections and clean the kingpin pads. Adding a small dab of conductive grease there ensures good electrical contact.

I check all of the axle bearings and remove any pet hair or stringy lint that's wrapped itself around the axle. Then I wipe off any excess oil that may have spread around inside the model.

Most models have plenty of lubrication, so I seldom add any more unless a gearbox is obviously dry or an axle is squeaking. An occasional tiny drop of plastic-compatible oil on the motor

bearings is usually all that's required to keep them well lubricated.

Repairs

Repairs are the last phase of my annual inspection. I carefully go over the carbody and make sure all of the details are securely fastened. An occasional drop of cyanoacrylate adhesive can do wonders here. Then I reassemble the body on the chassis.

My last step is to check the couplers for proper height and operation without drooping. Since engine couplers take a lot of pounding, I replace any that don't work perfectly and make sure their coupler boxes are fastened securely and parallel with the railheads. I've also found a small puff of graphite or powdered Teflon in the coupler box helps keep them working smoothly.

These tests and adjustments only take a few minutes, but they pay off in a smoother running railroad.

Open handrail holes with reamers

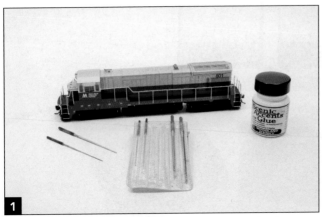

1 The mounting pins on modeler-installed handrails may not fit into their openings straight from the box. Reamers are a quick and easy way to enlarge the openings to the correct size.

2 Insert the reamer into the opening and give it two or three twists. Test fit the handrails as you work so the openings don't get too big.

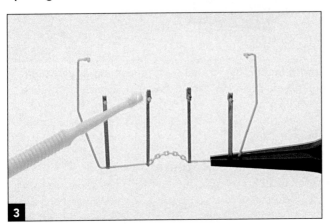

3 Pressure-sensitive adhesive, like Woodland Scenics Scenic Accent glue, holds the handrails in place without damaging the model.

4 A pair of smooth-jaw needlenose pliers makes it easy to install the handrails without damaging the plastic.

One common problem with locomotives that include modeler-installed handrails is that the openings for the mounting pins aren't big enough. This can often be attributed to paint filling the holes. Instead of trying to force handrails into too small of an opening, you can use reamers to make the holes larger, **1**. I use Mascot Precision Tools six-piece reamer set no. 311. Each reamer is tapered, so the hole gets larger the farther you push it into the opening.

For this project, I needed to install the front and rear handrails on an Atlas HO scale General Electric B23-7. After inserting the reamer, I gave it two or three twists, **2**. I repeated this process for the rest of the openings. I test-fit the handrails to make sure the mounting pins fit snuggly into the openings. It's easy to make the holes too big, and fixing oversized holes is difficult.

Before installing the handrails, I used a Microbrush to apply a small amount of Woodland Scenics Scenic Accent glue to the mounting pins, **3**. This pressure-sensitive adhesive comes out of the bottle white but dries clear and tacky. The glue holds the handrails in place yet allows them to be removed without damaging the model.

Finally, I pressed the handrails into the openings with a pair of smooth-jaw needlenose pliers, **4**. Don't use pliers with serrated jaws as they can damage the handrails.

Remove and replace molded details

1 I replaced the molded grab irons on the Accurail car in the foreground with wire details. The car in the background has molded details.

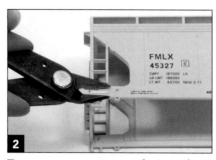

2 To save some extra work, I used sprue cutters to remove a large portion of each grab iron.

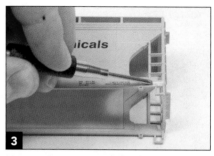

3 Use a Mission Models Micro Chisel to remove the rest of the plastic. Work slowly and in light passes to not damage the plastic carbody.

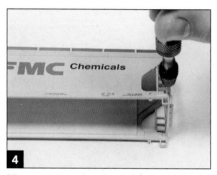

4 Next, use a pin vise with a no. 80 bit to drill openings for the grab irons.

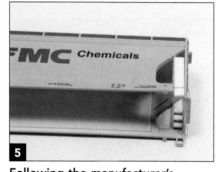

5 Following the manufacturer's instructions, I used a piece of .030" styrene as a spacer for the grab iron.

6 I finished by painting the handrails and touching up the plastic with Polly Scale Southern Pacific Light Gray.

We're fortunate to have an abundance of good-looking, well-detailed models to pick from today. However, we can make these models even better by removing molded details and replacing them with freestanding parts, as I did on an Accurail HO scale FMC Chemical American Car & Foundry Center Flow covered hopper, **1**.

On this Accurail hopper, I wanted to replace the molded grab irons with wire replacement parts. First, I used a pair of sprue cutters to clip off a large chunk of each grab iron, **2**. This made it easier to remove the rest of the material with a Mission Models Micro Chisel, **3**. I made several light passes with the chisel

instead of trying to remove all the material at once. This reduced the chances that I'd gouge the model.

I preserved the nut-bolt-washer detail for each grab iron and used that as a guide for drilling holes for the wire grab irons with a no. 80 bit, **4**. The bit is delicate, so don't force it or apply excess pressure when drilling.

After drilling the holes, I installed Detail Associates 19½" drop-style grab irons on the sides, 22" drop-style on the ends, and 22" straight for the running board corners. I secured the metal details with cyanoacrylate adhesive (CA). I used a piece of .030" styrene as a spacer while the CA cured, **5**. Then, I trimmed the excess grab iron legs with wire cutters.

I finished the model by painting the grab irons and touching up the exposed plastic with Polly Scale Southern Pacific Light Gray, **6**.

Removing molded details may sound daunting, but it isn't. If you take your time and use the right tools, you can make a good-looking model even better.

CODY SAYS:

When installing the grab irons on the lower parts of the car, cut the legs flush with the car's interior. If you don't, the underframe will not seat properly.

Install a distinctive nose bell

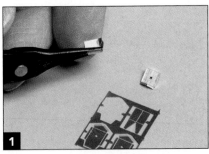

1 Each Plano etching includes three inserts and a template for the opening in the nose. Use a pair of smooth-jaw needlenose pliers to shape the parts.

2 With the template centered and pressed tightly on the nose and against the sand filler, use a pencil to carefully mark the insert's location.

3 With a pin vise, drill a starter hole somewhere inside the template's outline. The size of the starter hole isn't important.

4 Next, use a sharp no. 11 blade to gently enlarge the starter hole. The plastic is soft, so it's easy to carve the necessary opening.

5 As you get close to the pencil lines, test-fit a shaped insert in the opening. Complete any final sizing with a flat needle file to obtain a snug fit.

6 Secure the brass plate with CA. After the CA sets, paint the insert and add a Detail Associates gong bell.

Signature details make a big difference in the appearance and realism of model locomotives, especially if they're items that aren't applied by the manufacturer. In this case, I was thrilled when Atlas released ready-to-run HO scale GP40 models decorated for my favorite prototype Detroit, Toledo & Ironton RR. These models included just about every detail I was looking for except the DT&I's distinctive nose bell.

Fortunately, Plano released a etched brass detail set that simplified the installation of the bell, **1**. Each set included three inserts and a template for the nose opening. I shaped the inserts with a smooth-jaw needlenose pliers. Then I centered the template on the nose and marked the insert's position, **2**.

I drilled a starter hole with a pin vise through the upper corner of the future opening, **3**. Although I used a no. 50 bit, the size of the starter hole isn't important. Next, I carefully enlarged the starter hole in the soft plastic with a hobby knife and sharp no. 11 blade, **4**. As I neared the template's edges, I test-fit an insert and adjusted the opening with a flat needle file, **5**.

I used cyanoacrylate adhesive (CA) to fasten the brass insert, **6**. I then painted the insert and attached a Detail Associates no. 1204 gong bell.

After I added the distinctive DT&I nose bells to my GP40s, it was truly amazing how different the models looked. When the prototypes were delivered, the nose bells were painted silver. But as the locomotives were repainted, the bells usually were sprayed orange. I decided to paint my bells silver to make them stand out more.

Some of the former DT&I units were hastily repainted into Grand Trunk Western's blue, orange, and white scheme shortly after the merger. A few retained their gong bells in the new paint scheme, but most of these unusual bells disappeared as the GTW rebuilt the former DT&I locomotives.

Clean locomotive wheels

1 Paper towels and 70 percent isopropyl alcohol are all you need for cleaning locomotive wheelsets.

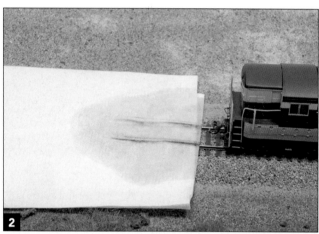

2 Place a paper towel over the tracks and wet it (but don't soak it) with isopropyl alcohol. Let the model start running, and then hold it in place and let the wheels spin for a few seconds.

3 After just a few seconds of running, the towel picks up a lot of dirt and gunk that impede a locomotive's ability to run smoothly.

4 Offset the wet towel and repeat the process for the rear truck. Then run the wheelsets over a dry towel when you're finished.

Over time, a locomotive's wheelsets will gather dirt and other gunk that will affect its ability to run smoothly, but regular wheel cleaning keeps your steam or diesel locomotives running at their peak. By using 70 percent isopropyl alcohol and a paper towel, two items that you most likely have in your house, you can give your engine a quick cleaning that greatly improves its performance, **1**.

First, I set some paper towel on the tracks. Then I use a pipette to apply some isopropyl alcohol to the towel (wet but not soaked), **2**. Next, I run the locomotive on the alcohol-soaked towel and let it build up some speed. I hold the locomotive and let the wheels spin for a few seconds. As you can see in photo **3**, there's quite a bit of dirt on the towel.

I offset the wet towel and clean the rear trucks, **4**. If you don't offset the towel (or use a new one), you'll just spread the dirt onto the other wheels. To finish, run the wheelsets over a dry towel.

CODY SAYS:

Cleaning the rails regularly helps cut down the amount of dirt and gunk that accumulates on locomotive wheelsets.

Repair and paint acetal handrails

1 Acetal plastic handrails are common on today's ready-to-run locomotives. If they break, you can repair them with Loctite's plastics bonding system.

2 Loctite's plastics bonding system consists of an activator/primer and glue. Once the handrails are clean and dry, apply the activator to both sides of the break and let it dry.

3 Next, apply the glue to one side of the break. A super fine (white) Microbrush or a toothpick makes for a handy glue applicator.

4 Hold the joint for 30 seconds, being careful to keep the glue off your skin.

Most recent ready-to-run locomotives use acetal (sometimes called *slippery* or *engineering*) plastic handrails. These handrails feature a scale profile and fine detail, but they're also prone to snapping. Traditional liquid plastic cement and cyanoacrylate adhesive will not bond acetal plastic, but Loctite's plastics bonding system will, **1**. This two-part system makes it easy to fix broken handrails in less than two minutes. It is available at most hardware stores and home supply centers. The pack contains an activator/primer and glue. Here's how it works.

Using the bonding system

The handrails need to be clean and dry before making the repair. Once they are, apply the activator/primer to both sides of the break, and let it dry for 1 minute, **2**. Then sparingly apply the glue to one side of the break, **3**. A toothpick or a super fine (white)

5 To match the prototype, I painted the vertical railings on my HO scale Dakota, Minnesota & Eastern GP9s with remote-control car paint. The flexible paint works well on acetal plastic.

6 Pactra, Faskolor, and Badger are three firms that offer flexible paint designed for remote-control car bodies. All three brands produce acrylic paint, and Pactra also has an organic solvent-based line.

7 To give the yellow an even finish, I first applied Pactra Sprint White over the blue plastic. Two coats may be necessary for complete coverage.

8 After the white paint had dried, I applied Bright Yellow to the railings.

Microbrush works well in applying the glue. Hold the joint together for 30 seconds, being careful not to get the glue on your fingers, **4**. According to the manufacturer's instructions, if you bond your fingers, apply cooking oil to the area and gently roll your fingers back and forth until they separate.

Painting the handrails

Just as the plastic requires special glue to repair breaks, it also requires specially formulated paint that's flexible and won't flake off. Fortunately, the paint is most likely available at the same hobby shop where you purchase your trains. Flexible paint designed for remote-control (RC) car bodies is the

perfect solution for locomotive handrails. RC paint is offered in a limited number of colors compared to model railroad paint, but it can be mixed to yield the color you need.

To match the prototype, I needed to paint the vertical railings on my HO scale Dakota, Minnesota & Eastern Electro-Motive Division GP9s, **5**. Although the railings were molded in blue plastic to match the locomotives' body color, the vertical railings, which are painted yellow on the full-size engines to increase crew visibility, were also blue. Most vertical railings on locomotives are painted silver, white, or yellow, but it's always good practice to check prototype photographs before committing paint to your model.

To remedy this, I turned to RC paint, **6**. Badger Air-Brush, Faskolor, and Pactra, among others, offer acrylic (water-based) RC paint. Pactra also produces an organic solvent-based line. From this line, I used Sprint White and Bright Yellow for my DM&E Geeps. You might be asking, "Why two colors?" A white undercoat makes it easier for the yellow to cover in fewer coats.

I brush-painted the vertical railings white (silver would also work), **7**. For best results, the paint should completely cover the railings and form a "jacket" around the part. Once the white had dried, I applied the yellow, **8**. Since the Pactra paint is solvent based, I worked in a well-ventilated area and wore nitrile gloves.

SCENERY

Scenery is often the element that separates an okay model railroad from a great layout. Though we often limit scenery to ground cover and trees, I consider it to be all of the elements that make up a scene. With the products available today, it's easy to model tall grass in a variety of colors, have trees with fine armatures and wood trunks, and re-create murky water with two-part resin.

If you're looking for the basics of ground cover, I've got that covered on pages 57–59. For those looking to take their scenery to the next level, other projects include how to model a modern grade crossing, cast plaster rocks, make gravel roads, and add car stops.

Whether you're just starting the scenery on your model railroad or adding the finishing touches, give these techniques a try. I know you'll be happy with the results.

Add mounting pins to fence sections

Central Valley's plastic fence lacks mounting pins, making it difficult to install on extruded-foam insulation board. However, with brass mounting pins, the fence can easily be pressed into place.

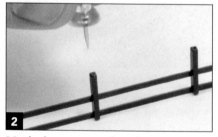

Mark the center of each post with a push pin. The dimple prevents the drill bit from wandering.

Use a drill with a no. 69 drill bit marked 1 scale foot from the tip to drills holes to a consistent depth.

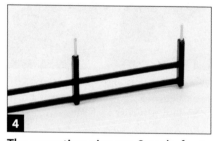

The mounting pins are 2 scale foot lengths of .028" brass wire. Attach them with medium viscosity CA.

Central Valley's HO scale injection-molded plastic fence is a close match for the fence used by the Burlington Northern near buildings in the area of Minnesota that I model, **1**. Though the fence looks good, it's difficult to attach as-is to an extruded-foam insulation scenery base. However, with brass mounting pins, the fence can easily be pressed into place.

The first step in adding mounting pins is to mark the center of each post. With a push pin, I put a dimple at the center point in the bottom of each post, **2**. This prevents the drill bit from wandering.

Next, I measured 1 scale foot from the tip of a no. 69 drill bit and put masking tape at that location, **3**. The tape acts as a stop, so all of the holes are drilled to the same depth.

After inserting the bit into a pin vise, I began drilling the holes, keeping the bit as vertical as possible. If the bit hesitated, I would back it out to clean out the plastic shavings before finishing the hole. It's important to let the bit do

the work. If you force the pin vise, you may snap the delicate drill bit.

With all of the holes drilled, I began installing the brass mounting pins. I used 2 scale foot lengths of .028" brass wire for the pins, **4**. I installed them with medium viscosity cyanoacrylate adhesive (CA).

On a short length of fence, only three pins are necessary: at the end posts and middle post. After the CA had dried, I painted and weathered the fence. Installation was a matter of pressing the fence into the foam scenery base.

Make a forest of puff-ball trees

1 Tease a 4" tuft of poly fiber to the size of a golf ball. Dip it into a 50/50 mix of white glue and water to dampen the poly fiber clump.

2 Roll the wet poly fiber ball into one or more colors of ground foam. Don't worry if the foam doesn't stick to all of the fibers.

3 To simulate new leaves, roll the balls quickly in Scenic Express light green foam.

4 Waiting on a plastic paint tray to be planted, the trees look like moldy meatballs, but on the layout they will look like a forest.

5 The still-damp trees are easy to position in groups, and when the glue dries, it locks the puff balls together. This photo shows the completed forest on the layout.

Because *Model Railroader*'s Virginian project railroad is set in the Appalachian Mountains of West Virginia, we had to model a tightly packed deciduous forest, which translated to a huge number of trees. We figured that we could speed things up by using the old practice of making puff-ball trees, which models just the treetops without the trunks and branches.

Puff-ball trees aren't new, but they sure are effective and are among the least expensive ways to fill a landscape with trees. We made a few trees with green poly fiber, but found that black fiber makes a big visual difference. We continued with black poly fiber from Micro-Mark.

To begin, take a 4" tuft of poly fiber and tease it into a rough shape about the size of a golf ball, **1**. Then dip it into a 50/50 mix of white glue and water. Squeeze out the excess so the poly fiber is wet but not soaked.

Next, roll the wet poly fiber ball into ground foam, **2**. We used two colors—first Woodland Scenics blended green and then burnt grass. Don't worry if the foam doesn't stick to all of the fibers. Then, we gave each puff ball a quick roll in Scenic Express light green foam to simulate new leaves, **3**. By sticking to this pattern—blended green, burnt grass, and light green—all the trees looked consistent.

We put the damp puff balls into a plastic paint tray, **4**. These disposable tray liners worked great for holding a large number of puff balls. Then we planted the damp trees using full-strength white glue. We learned that puff balls are best planted while they are still damp, as they can be teased out and nestled together far more easily than when dry.

To break up the sameness of the puff balls, we planted a few Scenic Express trees, coated with the same colors of ground foam for consistency, on the layout, **5**.

Uncover the basics of ground cover

Ground foam turf, static grass, and foliage clumps are just three types of ground cover used to complete this scene on the HO scale Milwaukee, Racine & Troy.

You're in the scenery aisle at your local hobby shop, and you see bags with products labeled static grass, lichen, and ground foam, among others. You start wondering which products to purchase and how you can use them on your model railroad. I'll give you the basics here in getting started with ground cover.

Ground foam has been joined by new materials such as static grass; laser-cut paper weeds; and scenery mats that model ponds, farm fields, and cow pastures, **1**. There is also an assortment of products available to secure scenery materials to your lay-out. Most scenery manufacturers offer

their own line of scenery glue, or you can also make your own by diluting white glue or matte medium with water.

When in doubt about how scenery should look, refer to prototype photos. And if you don't like how a scene looks, don't be afraid to give it another try.

Landforms

The portion of the MR&T I scenicked had plaster-impregnated gauze strips over a web of cardboard strips. However, before I could start adding

scenery, I had to cover a 2 x 6-inch opening that wasn't filled in when the original scenery base was built.

I covered the hole with pieces of plaster gauze. After the plaster dried, I used Sculptamold, a papier-mache-like product, to add contours to the scene. I let the Sculptamold dry completely, so there were no cold, damp spots, before proceeding.

Finally, I painted the plaster and Sculptamold with flat tan latex paint that I thinned with water (heavier than a wash and but not quite full-strength

After covering the hole with plaster gauze, I added contours to the scene with Sculptamold, and painted the area with flat tan latex paint thinned with water.

To attach the scenery material to the base, I first brushed on thinned white glue and then sprinkled on the four shades of foam turf.

I then sprayed the turf with 70 percent isopropyl alcohol and followed it with a thorough application of Scenic Cement using a pipette.

To fill in the right-of-way and give it some realistic texture, I planted some foliage clusters, light green foliage, and tufts of Busch late summer grass.

paint), **2**. Instead of tan, you can substitute a color more appropriate to the area you're modeling.

Ground foam turf

I built up the scenery in layers, starting with ground foam turf. Since the scenery was complete to the left and right of where I was working, I needed to match the ground foam's existing colors: Woodland Scenics earth blend, green blend, yellow grass, and soil turf.

There are different schools of thought on attaching scenery material. Some people prefer applying the turf directly to wet paint on the base.

While this is okay, the ground foam will absorb the paint color. For this project, I applied thinned white glue (nine parts glue, one part water) to the scenery base and sprinkled on the foam, **3**.

After I applied the four shades of turf to the base, I sprayed the area with 70 percent isopropyl alcohol. I let the alcohol soak in for two minutes before applying Woodland Scenics Scenic Cement with a pipette, **4**. The alcohol helps the Scenic Cement wick through the ground foam. When you can see the white through the foam, you know it's thoroughly saturated with adhesive.

Adding texture

The railroad right-of-way is an often overlooked scenic opportunity, **5**. Though full-size railroads keep weeds and tall grass trimmed back, the right-of-way is by no means manicured like a golf course.

To give the MR&T some realistic texture, I started by randomly attaching Woodland Scenics light green foliage clusters with full-strength white glue. The ground foam clusters are offered in three shades of green and work well for bushes and undergrowth.

Next, I used Woodland Scenics light green foliage to simulate weeds and other low growth. This material can be teased apart to cover large areas such as a hillside or forest floor.

I completed scenicking the trackside scene by planting tufts of Busch late summer grass. The grass is sold in 8 x 11-inch sheets and has a self-adhesive backing material. However, I applied full-strength white glue to the backs of the tufts to be sure they would remain fixed to the landscape.

Static grass

I wanted the hillside to look unkempt. A fence with crooked posts and long-abandoned vehicles help reinforce that theme, but so would static grass.

What is static grass? It's dyed rayon-based fibers that stand on end when applied in wet scenic cement with an electrostatic applicator. I used the Noch Gras-Master for this project, but the Heki Flockstar (available from Scenic Express) will also work.

Static grass is offered in various heights and colors from different manufacturers. For this project, I applied it in layers. First, I used the Noch Gras-Master to apply Woodland Scenics 2mm harvest gold grass flock, **6**. I followed that with Busch 6mm dark green and spring green fibers.

As nice as static grass is, it can look too uniform when applied over a large area, so after the Scenic Cement had dried, I applied Bachmann spring green turf and Scenic Express aspen yellow turf, **7**.

I secured it to the layout by spraying it with 70 percent isopropyl alcohol, letting the alcohol soak in for two minutes, and then applying Woodland Scenics Scenic Cement with a pipette.

Bare soil

Not every square inch of landscape should be covered with grass. I simulated erosion on the hillside with Scenic Express fine natural soil, **8**. I sprinkled the soil over the static grass and used a paintbrush to sweep it in between the static grass fibers. I let some of the soil roll into the ballast and down the hillside, just as it would in real life.

If scenery has you stumped, give these products and techniques a try. Soon you'll be scenicking your model railroad with confidence.

To help give the hillside a less-groomed look, I applied several layers of static grass with a Noch Gras-Master that I grounded to a T-pin. Damp towels keep the fibers off the rails and ballast.

To break up the uniformity of the static grass, I added some green and yellow foam turf with a plastic spoon, gently tapping it to spread the turf. This suggests coarse weeds growing in the grass.

For a final realistic touch, I added some Scenic Express soil to the hill to simulate erosion. This should be applied after the glue for the static grass has dried.

Create a quiet grade crossing

1

You'd expect the air horns to be blasting when trains approach a grade crossing, but not at this quiet grade crossing on the Milwaukee, Racine & Troy, which also is a visually interesting location.

Adding a quiet zone to your layout gives your model railroad an up-to-date appearance, as I did on *Model Railroader*'s Milwaukee, Racine & Troy layout, **1**. Now you might be asking, "I have bunch of sound-equipped locomotives. Why would I want a quiet zone on my layout?" Well, they're a part of today's railroad scene. Having a quiet grade crossing or two on your model railroad will keep operators on their toes, as they have to pay attention to where they can and cannot sound a locomotive's air horn.

Quiet zones aren't interesting just from an operating perspective. The slightly raised median and vertical markers, both bright yellow, make the approach to grade crossings visually interesting.

Installing a quiet grade crossing doesn't require a lot of materials. Styrene strip, channel, and half round; crossing gates (with arms) of your choice; and some road material are all you need to get started.

Of course, if you have an existing grade crossing, the project will go even quicker. In a few evenings, you can give your model railroad some modern flavor with a quiet zone.

Paving the road

I used Busch foam asphalt highway material for the road. The foam material has a peel-and-stick back, so it needs a smooth surface for good adhesion. For the base, I used .040" styrene sheet. The

2

I put down .040" styrene sheet as a smooth base to provide good adhesion for the Busch foam asphalt highway material, which has a peel-and-stick back.

3

After the road has been positioned, use a wallpaper roller to smooth out irregularities and help ensure even adhesion of the road material to the styrene.

4

I installed BLMA rubber grade crossing strips, which are easy to cut and fit the irregular track angles found in the crossing.

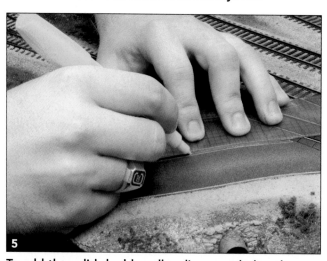

5

To add the solid double yellow lines needed at the grade crossing, I used a plastic rule and a Sharpie poster-paint marker.

adhesive is very tacky, so you only get one chance to stick the road material down, **2**.

Once I had the road in place, I used a wallpaper roller to smooth out irregularities, **3**. This helps ensure good, even adhesion of the road material to the styrene. If you do get air bubbles or wrinkles in the foam, slit them with a knife to release the air and then smooth them with the roller.

Grade crossing

Rubber mats, wood planks, and concrete are three common styles of grade crossings used today. Several manufacturers make grade crossing kits in HO scale, including Accurail, Blair Line, BLMA, GC Laser, and Walthers.

For this project, I installed BLMA's rubber grade crossing strips, **4**. The injection-molded plastic pieces have raised detail like the prototype, and they are easy to cut—with a razor saw or hobby knife—and file. This was important because, as you can see, the crossing has some interesting track angles.

Next, I cut pieces of .040" styrene to fit between the grade crossing strips. I glued the styrene to the strips using Tenax-7R. I then brush-painted the styrene with Polly Scale Union Pacific Dark Gray before applying the Busch road material. The gray closely matches the color of the road, making gaps between the road and the grade crossing less visible.

Pavement markings

The Busch asphalt highway has dashed white lines down the middle, great for two-lane roads but incorrect for a grade crossing. I needed solid double yellow lines. To do this, I used a plastic rule and a yellow Sharpie poster-paint marker with an extra-fine tip, **5**. Since the foam is porous, the paint bled some. I wasn't too concerned about this, since not all road striping is perfect. Besides, most of the stripes would be covered by median separators.

To prevent the paint from wicking under the rule, put a few pieces of masking tape or a thin strip of cork on the underside. Set the material in about ⅛" from the edge that you'll be using as a guide.

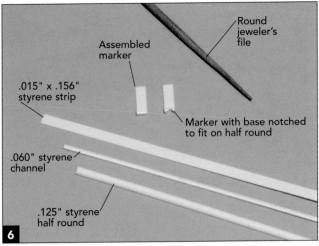

.015" x .156" styrene strip

Assembled marker

Round jeweler's file

Marker with base notched to fit on half round

.060" styrene channel

.125" styrene half round

6

I constructed median separators out of simple styrene pieces. I cut the strips into markers and notched their bases with a round jeweler's file.

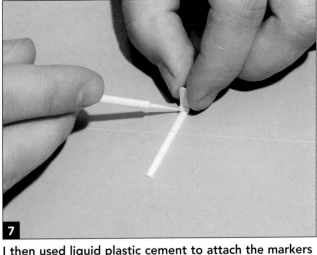

7

I then used liquid plastic cement to attach the markers to the .125" half round. The markers should be perpendicular to the base.

8

I painted the median separators yellow, building the paint up layers to provide the best coverage, let them dry overnight, and then attached the chevrons.

9

Finishing details include highway grade crossing signals, an electric relay cabinet, and white stop lines on the road.

Median separators

The key element of this project is the median separators. Mine are simple affairs, made of .125" styrene half round, .060" styrene channel, and .015" x .156" styrene strip, **6**.

To model the markers, I first cut lengths of .015" x .156" styrene strip. The prototype marker panels, without base, are 34⅛" tall. I used chevrons in Blair Line's HO scale traffic sign pack no. 110 as the guide for the height of my markers.

Next, I lightly glued the marker panels to the back of the .060" channel with liquid plastic cement. Yes, I only modeled half of the base, but only one side of the median separator is visible in the crossing scene at Mukwonago.

After using a round jeweler's file to notch the base of each marker, I used liquid plastic cement to attach the markers to the .125" half round, **7**. The markers are spaced 3 scale feet apart.

Next, I painted the median separators. I first primed the styrene with Rust-Oleum Gray Automobile Primer, so the final colors would cover evenly. Once the primer had dried, I used an airbrush to paint the separators Polly Scale Signal Yellow. Since yellow doesn't always cover well, I built the paint up in numerous layers instead of trying to get sufficient coverage in two or three coats. I let paint dry overnight before attaching the chevrons with double-sided tape, **8**. Then I attached the medians to the road

with medium-viscosity cyanoacrylate adhesive.

Final details

To finish the scene, I installed N.J. International highway grade crossing signals (no. 1162), **9**. Since the road here is at an angle, I used a pair of smooth-jaw needlenose pliers to carefully twist the post on which the crossbucks and flashers are attached. This allowed the gates to be parallel to the tracks.

Then I installed a Details West electric relay cabinet. I also added white stop lines a scale 8 feet in front of the crossing gate arm. [The lines may be a bit short and too thin. I'll have to extend them from the median to the white stripe on the edge of the road.]

Cast rocks in place

A rocky outcropping replaces an unnaturally steep dirt embankment.

I used a putty knife to remove most of the old ground cover from the embankment.

I followed up with a hand brush to clean loose ground cover from the plaster.

In model railroading, building upon someone else's work is usually meant in the figurative sense—a hobbyist is inspired to make an even better version of something that someone else created first.

For the rock castings shown in photo **1**, I literally built upon someone else's work. Near the back of the serpentine Milwaukee, Racine & Troy, the *Model Railroader*'s club layout, is a river bridge erected by a long-ago employee.

The bridge and its abutment still look great, but the steep curved embankment adjacent to the abutment has always needed something more. When the patches of old, dried-up lichen were removed from this part of the layout several years ago, the embankment's geological shortcomings were even clearer.

To remedy the situation, I added rock castings made from Hydrocal plaster and colored them to match the outcroppings on the far bank of the river. Because the surface selected for

the castings is slightly curved, some of the rocks had to be cast in place. When casting plaster rocks in place, the rocks are positioned before the mold plaster is fully cured, allowing the entire rock to more naturally fit an irregular surface.

This technique isn't much different than casting plaster rocks on your workbench. The only trick is timing: the plaster-filled mold must be solid enough to be handled and held upright, yet the partially cured plaster needs to be flexible enough to wrap around a contour before it fully sets, which doesn't always work right the first time.

Plaster and paint

For this project, I used Woodland Scenics rock molds, Hydrocal, and its earth color kit, which contains a sampling of pigments from stone gray to burnt umber. The pigment variety will help tint these rocks a color that closely matches the slate-colored rocks across the layout's river. Work began on this

layout in the late 1980s, so the color mix of those older rocks has been lost to time. To blend our new rocks into the existing landscape, I used lightweight Hydrocal casting plaster. Although using Sculptamold may seem to make more sense, it takes paints and pigments differently than casting plaster.

Cleaning the surface

I needed to clean the embankment before casting the rocks. I used a putty knife and a hand brush to remove loose ground cover and related scenery material from the existing plaster surface, **2** and **3**. Then, I used a can of compressed air (the same type designed to clean computer keyboards) to blow away dirt and dust from the surface.

Mixing and pouring

Depending on the style of rubber mold you choose, you can cast one or multiple rocks at the same time. I used a random rock mold (no. 1234) to make the two larger rocks.

4 After misting the plaster with water, I held the molds in place until the plaster set.

5 I filled gaps in the plaster with smaller rocks and Hydrocal, which I applied with my fingers.

6 Using burnt umber pigment, I matched the color of the rocks on the other side of the river.

7 After adding an India ink wash to the rocks, I dry-brushed the edges to highlight them more.

8 To hold new ground foam to the steep slope, I brushed on diluted white glue.

9 I then applied full-strength white glue to attach foilage clusters.

After mixing a small batch of Hydrocal plaster, I sprayed the mold with "wet" water (water with a few drops of liquid dish detergent added). Then I poured the mixture into the two mold sections. The plaster mixes better if you add dry plaster to the water, not the other way around.

Placing the rocks

Just before the plaster was completely set, I carried the molds from the workbench to the embankment, misted the embankment with water from a pump sprayer. I held the molds in place for about 10 minutes until the plaster had set and would stay in place by itself, **4**.

After an hour passed, I carefully peeled off the mold. As I was peeling away the mold, I noticed a few voids in the casting. Instead of removing the casting and making a new one, I filled the voids with Hydrocal.

It took a couple of attempts for the castings to work. The first time, I waited too long before placing the mold, and as a result, the Hydrocal was too dry, and it broke apart within the mold when placed onto the curve. When I removed the mold, the Hydrocal crumbled. To avoid this mistake, try a few experimental rocks to determine your best timing.

Filling in the gaps

Anticipating some gaps to fill, I used a layered rock mold (no. 1241) to produce several smaller rocks at the workbench rather than casting them in place. Once these dried overnight, I began the trial-and-error process of fitting the shapes into the voids on the embankment. I used a hammer and chisel to carefully break some of the rocks into smaller pieces. I filled gaps using different size pieces and changed their orientation to avoid any unnatural repetition, **5**. I adhered these pieces to the embankment with latex adhesive caulk. Once all of the rocks were in place, I filled the remaining gaps with Hydrocal using a 1" putty knife and my fingers to apply the material.

Matching colors

I applied two coats of Burnt Umber pigment to build up a color that reasonably matched the existing brown-gray rocks on the other side of the river, **6**. After they dried, I finished the rocks with a wash of India ink (2 teaspoons of ink diluted in 1 pint of 70 percent isopropyl alcohol). The black wash settled into the rock cracks to emphasize the texture and shadows.

I highlighted the edges of the rocks by drybrushing them (removing most of the paint from the brush before applying it to the casting), **7**. I used four Polly Scale colors (Sand, Rust, Mineral Red, and Louisville & Nashville Gray) to try to match the existing rocks.

Final touches

Once I was satisfied with the color of the new rocks, it was time for the final touch: adding ground foam to match the colors and textures of the existing landscape on this part of the layout. I scenicked the area with Woodland Scenics products.

Since the embankment slopes steeply, I applied diluted white glue (nine parts glue to one part water) with a brush, **8**. With the glue still wet, I sprinkled on the ground foam. Later, I used full-strength white glue to attach the foliage clusters, representing bushes and undergrowth, **9**.

As a final touch, I used O scale ballast to simulate small chips of rock that had broken off and rolled to the base of the embankment.

Add gravel parking lots and roads

1

The parking lot next to the crew office is made of Highball Products Real Dirt. The granules are roughly the size of N scale ballast, which is appropriate for HO scale gravel.

When you think of modeling gravel roads and parking lots in HO scale, you may think of using 1:87.1 proportion ballast for the road surface. Though the ballast captures the look of gravel, the granules are too big for HO scale gravel. Instead, try using Highball Products Real Dirt. The material is ground to the consistency of N scale ballast.

For this scene, I modeled a gravel parking lot next to a crew office, **1**. The scenery base is extruded-foam insulation board. To prevent the pink foam

from showing through the scenery, I painted it with a flat earth-toned latex paint, **2**. Don't use an organic solvent-based paint as it will dissolve the foam.

Next, I applied thinned white glue (nine parts glue to one part water) on the driveway with a paintbrush, **3**. It's important to work in manageable sections, so the glue doesn't dry out before the scenery can be applied.

With the glue still wet, I applied a thin layer of Real Dirt, **4**. The material was a bit too uniform for my taste, so I sprinkled in some Highball Products N scale limestone ballast, **5**.

I let the glue dry for about 10 minutes before I wet the area with 70 percent isopropyl alcohol, **6**. The alcohol breaks the surface tension of the scenery material, making it easier for the scenery glue to wick all the way through. I let the alcohol soak for 5 minutes.

Finally, I applied Woodland Scenics Scenic Cement with a pipette, **7**. You know the material is sufficiently wet when you can see white between the granules. I let the glue dry overnight before adding the crew office and fence (see page 55).

2

To prevent pink foam from showing through, paint the scenery base with a flat earth-toned latex paint. Make sure you don't use solvent-based paint as it will dissolve the foam.

3

Use an old paintbrush to apply thinned white glue. Work in manageable sections, so the glue doesn't dry before the scenery is added.

4

A spoon makes a handy applicator for the Real Dirt, which becomes the main color for the parking lot.

5

To break up the uniform color of the Real Dirt, I sprinkled in Highball Products N scale limestone ballast.

6

Wet the ballast with 70 percent isopropyl alcohol to break the surface tension of the real rock material, making it easier for the scenery glue to wick through.

7

I used Woodland Scenics Scenic Accent Glue to secure the granules. Once you can see white through the granules, you know the area is thoroughly soaked.

Model water with two-part resin

On the Milwaukee, Racine & Troy, GP38 no. 834 leads a cut of grain hoppers across the scratchbuilt ballasted-deck bridge, as detailed on pages 68–69, and over the newly modeled water that completes the harbor scene.

Scenes where rails meet the water have a lot of wow factor on a model railroad. On the *Model Railroader* HO scale Milwaukee, Racine & Troy club layout, one major water scene is the Milwaukee Harbor. The harbor is shown on a backdrop, but lacked physical features including water. Of course, a harbor scene on a model railroad wouldn't be complete without water, so I decided to detail the harbor with water, **1**.

For this project, I used Magic Water from Unreal Details. I'd never worked on a water project of this size using a two-part resin, so I was a bit nervous. However, by working carefully and following the manufacturer's instructions, everything went smoothly.

I added seawalls, bridges, a breakwater, and other details. Then I painted the bottom of the harbor with Rust-Oleum flat black latex paint, **2**. This area had been painted once before, but the color was faded and had stains from scenery glue and backdrop paint, leaving the area looking tired.

Before pouring the resin, I needed to install dams to contain the two-part

2 The bottom of the harbor had been painted previously but was stained and faded, so I repainted it with Rust-Oleum flat black latex paint.

3 To contain the resin, I installed styrene dams and caulked along the seam at the bottom of the harbor. I added clear styrene to protect the photo backdrop.

.015" clear styrene

.100" x .750" styrene strip

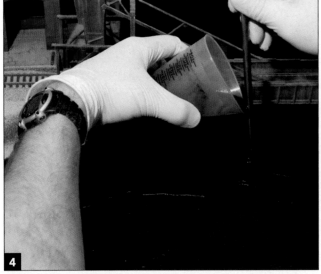

4 I tinted the resin black and poured it from a plastic cup, using a brass rod to guide the resin where I wanted it to go.

5 After the resin hardened, I applied Woodland Scenics Water Effects, working it in even rows to show waves moving across the harbor in one direction.

resin. I cut a piece of .015" clear styrene to protect the photo backdrop, **3**. Then I ran a bead of clear latex caulk along the seam between the styrene and the bottom of the harbor.

For the rest of the harbor, I made dams from .100" x .750" styrene strip. I used masking tape to temporarily hold the strips in place and then sealed the seam between the styrene and harbor with clear latex caulk.

I filled the harbor with the Magic Water. The material is self-leveling, so it's important that the area to be scenicked is flat. Though it's low-odor,

this two-part resin should be used in a well-ventilated area. I mixed 6-ounce batches in a disposable cup. When you first combine the two parts, the resin turns cloudy. I stirred the material with a short length of brass tubing for about 5 minutes. When the resin turns clear, it's ready to use. I then tinted each batch of resin with about 30 drops of Floquil Engine Black.

I used a brass rod to guide the resin where I wanted it to go, **4**. The rod also prevents the resin from splashing on the nearby scenery if it is poured straight from the cup. Though the

instructions say Magic Water will dry hard in 24 hours, these batches took a bit longer because of humidity.

Once the resin hardened, I applied Woodland Scenics Water Effects with a ½"-wide paintbrush, **5**. You can use this thick, paste-like material to create ripples in water and river rapids. A single coat of Water Effects makes small ripples and shallow waves, or you can apply the paste in layers to make rougher water. The material pours white but dries clear in a few hours. I worked it in even rows to suggest that the waves are moving across the harbor in one direction.

Build a ballasted-deck bridge

Spanning the Milwaukee Harbor is a ballasted-deck bridge that can easily be scratchbuilt from wood but made to look like concrete. The bridge abutment at right and the piers were constructed from stripwood.

To cross the water in *Model Railroader*'s Milwaukee Harbor scene, we used two different bridges: a lift bridge assembled from a kit, and a ballasted-deck bridge that I scratchbuilt from wood, **1**.

Scratchbuilding from wood is easy if you have the right supplies. Miter boxes and a razor saw are handy for cutting wood at angles. Both wood glue and cyanoacrylate adhesive (CA) work well for bonding wood. Other helpful items including sanding sticks, a rule, and a machinist's square.

Abutments and wings

I started the project by cutting the abutments and wings. To ensure the parts of the abutments will be at right angles and have clean cuts, use a miter box and a fine-tooth razor saw, **2**. Assemble the components with medium-viscosity CA

or wood glue. Use a clamp to hold the three-piece assembly together while the glue dries.

Depending on a location's terrain, the wings on prototype abutments can face backwards at an angle of 30 degrees or greater. Once you've marked the angle for the wings, use sanding sticks to shape the stripwood. Start with a coarse stick and then use medium and fine sticks for the final shaping.

The wings in our harbor scene angle downward, **3**, but to be prototypically correct, they should be flat and at the same height as the sheet piling. On full-size railroads, the wings angle down if the roadbed behind them does.

Trestle bents

Each trestle bent has a cap which transfers the load to the piles below. The caps on our bridge are 1¾" lengths

of ¼" x ⅜" stripwood. A piece of ¼"-diameter dowel serves as a handy guide to trace the end profile of the cap, **4**. Use sanding sticks to shape the wood.

After the caps are shaped, attach the three piles (¼"-diameter dowel cut to length) with CA or wood glue. Since the middle piles were glued into a hole drilled in the layout, it was cut longer, **5**. The outer piles were glued directly to the layout table.

Bridge deck and curbs

The bridge deck is a ⅜" x 2" mullion, which is available at most hardware stores and home centers. The mullion is 2" wide, so you'll need a large miter box to cut it.

Prototype ballasted-deck bridges have curbs to contain ballast. To re-create the slight lip between the curb and bridge deck, attach a piece of .020" styrene to

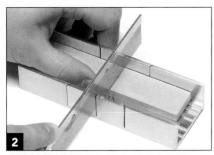

2

When making the abutment, use a miter box and a razor saw to keep the pieces at right angles.

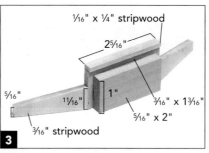

1/16" x 1/4" stripwood
2 5/16"
5/16"
11/16"
1"
3/16" x 1 3/16"
5/16" x 2"
3/16" stripwood

3

The finished abutment has the wing walls attached at a downward angle to fit under the lift bridge.

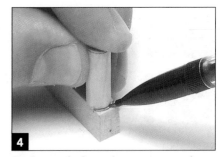

4

Each trestle bent has a cap, and a dowel piece serves as a guide to trace the end profile of the cap.

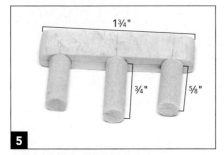

1 3/4"
3/4"
5/8"

5

Attach the piles with CA or wood glue. The middle pile fits into a hole so it is longer than the others.

6

To re-create the lip between the curb and bridge deck, attach 1/8" x 1/8" stripwood with CA.

7

Keep a scuff pad handy to remove any fuzz from the wood before spraying it with primer.

8

Attach the track with latex caulk or by pressing nails into pilot holes drilled into the ties.

9

After the track is in place, mask the bridge and spray the rails and ties with Polly Scale Railroad Tie Brown.

10

Apply Woodland Scenics Scenic Cement to secure the ballast between the rails and curbs.

a machinist's square with double-sided tape, **6**. Then press the bridge deck (mullion) against the styrene and attach 1/8" x 1/8" stripwood with CA.

Priming and painting

Once you have all of the bridge decks, abutments, wing walls, and bents assembled, mask any surfaces that will be glued (e.g. tops of the caps on the trestle bents). Then spray the parts with Rust-Oleum Gray Automobile Primer, **7**. This will ensure that the final color covers evenly. Let the primer dry for 24 hours before spraying the final color, which should simulate the concrete color of prototype bridges.

Track and ballast

Track can be installed using track nails or latex caulk. If using nails, drill pilot holes in the ties so you can press (not pound) the nails into the wood, **8**.

If your bridge is on a curve and you use latex caulk, you don't need to add nails, as the ballast (once glued down) will help hold the track in place.

With the track in place, mask the bridge and spray the rails and ties with Polly Scale Railroad Tie Brown, **9**. When the paint is still wet, wipe the rail heads with a cotton swab soaked in Windex. Any stubborn paint can be removed with lacquer thinner or an abrasive track cleaning block.

Once the paint dried for 24 hours, you can ballast the track. I used a 50:50 blend of Highball Products Light Gray and Dark Gray limestone ballast.

Spread the ballast between the rails with a 1/2"-paintbrush, making sure there are no granules on the tops of the ties or rail web. Then spray the ballast with 70 percent isopropyl alcohol and let it soak in for about 30 seconds. Finally, use a pipette to apply Woodland Scenics Scenic Cement, **10**. You know you've applied enough when you can see the Scenic Cement between the granules. Let the Scenic Cement dry, and then spread the ballast between the rails and curbs.

Install modern car-stopping devices

1 These Walthers HO scale bumping posts keep cars from rolling off the end of the rails on *Model Railroader*'s Wisconsin & Southern's Troy Yard.

If you look at model railroads, you might be convinced there are just one or two styles of car-stopping devices, **1**. However, that's far from the case. Here, I'll present some different examples of car stops that are used today and share some techniques for installing them.

It's often thought that bumping posts and wheel stops are meant to stop cars that are "kicked" (sent rolling) by a switchman, but they aren't. Instead, posts and stops are put in place for emergency situations so equipment doesn't roll off the end of the rails.

So what's the difference between the two? Well, bumping posts are sturdier and typically used at the ends of spurs and in passenger terminals. The Hayes bumping post has been used since before the 1930s and is still common today.

Wheel stops are designed for lighter duty, where speeds are less than 5 mph, such as the end of an industrial spur. The stops come in two styles, fixed and portable. Fixed wheel stops are bolted to the rails, while portable stops have braces that rest against the nearest tie and clamps that "grab" the rail when impacted by a wheel.

However, not all wheel stops are fancy. Some railroads use old ties as wheel stops. An even cheaper alterna-tive is to dump a pile of dirt, cinders, or ballast at the end of the line.

The bumping posts and wheel stops shown here aren't meant to be all-inclusive. Look at prototype photos to see what devices your favorite railroad used to keep cars from rolling away.

Bumping posts

The Hayes bumping post is available from several manufacturers, including Walthers and Tomar Industries. Though the Walthers and Tomar bumping posts are similar in appearance, the techniques for installing them are different.

The Walthers bumping post is an easy-to-assemble, injection-molded

This plastic Hayes bumping post from Walthers can be easily glued to the crossties with medium viscosity CA.

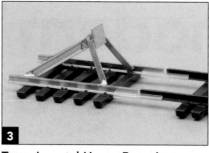

Tomar's metal Hayes Bumping post needs to be insulated before attaching it to the rails.

Prototype Buda wheel stops bolt to the rail web, but these Custom Finishing castings fit on the railhead.

Although made of metal, these Hayes type SF castings require no insulating gaps cut in the rails for installation.

A simple and inexpensive wheel stop made of crossties keeps slow-moving cars from rolling off the rails.

Painting embedded, car-stopping devices bright orange warns drivers to be aware of these objects.

plastic kit, **2**. However, before attaching it to the crossties with medium viscosity cyanoacrylate adhesive (CA), I carefully removed the molded spike detail on the ties with a no. 17 blade. Do this on the inside of the rails only, otherwise the rails will pop up.

The Hayes bumping post from Tomar Industries is factory assembled from brass stock and nickel silver rail, **3**. It's attached to a 1½"-long section of track. Since this bumper uses all-metal construction and is soldered to the rails, it will cause a short circuit unless electrically insulated.

To isolate the rails, you can either use the supplied insulated rail joiners or cut a gap in one of the two rails. If you use the latter technique, fill the gap with a piece of styrene. This will prevent the gap from closing if your benchwork contracts during humidity changes.

Wheel stops

Several manufacturers offer metal castings of fixed and portable wheel stops, including Tomar, Custom Finishing, and Selley Finishing Touches.

Buda wheel stops are based on prototypes that are bolted to the web of the rail, **4**. These Custom Finishing castings feature bolt detail for cosmetic purposes, but they simply fit onto the railhead (some filing may be necessary depending on the rail size you're using.) A drop or two of CA holds the castings to the railhead.

Since Hayes type SF wheel stops aren't generally bolted to the rail, they are considered portable—even though the real ones weigh 300 pounds each! The stop's edges clamp to the web of the rail, and the angled braces rest against the nearest crosstie.

Tomar's HO scale Hayes type SF castings can also be attached to the rail with CA, **5**. Though these and the Buda wheel stops in photo 4 are metal castings, no gaps need to be cut in the rail after installation.

Quick and dirty

Crossties are some of the oldest (and cheapest) forms of wheel stops. The ties aren't designed to stop cars rolling at a high rate of speed (the wheels would shear the ties). Instead, they

prevent slow-moving equipment from rolling off the end of the rails.

Regular MR contributor Paul Dolkos wedged two ties, crossed, under the rail so they rest on the railhead, **6**. Some railroads use an alternative version of this style by setting one or more ties on the railhead and securing them with bolts and steel bars.

Safety first

Most bumping posts and wheel stops are painted when they're new, but they turn a rusty brown color once they're exposed to the elements for a few years. However, some are painted high-visibility colors (typically yellow or orange) or have reflective striping added, so they're more visible in high-traffic areas.

For example, at Kalmbach Feeds on our HO scale Wisconsin & Southern project layout, wheel stops and a bumping post are located in a concrete lot with embedded rails. Since vehicles drive on this lot (including a tractor used to move cars), the car-stopping devices are painted bright orange to alert drivers to the obstacles, **7**.

PAINTING AND DECALING

Yes, I'll admit it. Painting and decaling are some of my most favorite aspects of the hobby. For me, there is nothing more rewarding than turning an unpainted locomotive, freight car, or structure into a realistic looking scale model.

Though I'm a proponent of using an airbrush for painting, I've also included techniques that can be done without this tool. I'll show you how to paint wheelsets with a Microbrush.

I'll also share some fun projects, such as making your own translucent paint using clear parts cement and food coloring and painting yellow freight cars. Oh, and if you have trouble with the caps on your paint jars being stuck, I've included some handy solutions for that too.

Learn the basics of airbrushing

Whether you're modeling a prototype railroad or operating a freelance line of your own creation, you want your equipment to look prototypical and have a sense of individuality. One way to achieve this goal is by painting your structures, freight cars, and locomotives with an airbrush. On the surface, airbrushing may seem like a difficult and intimidating task, but it really isn't. With practice, patience, and the right techniques, airbrushing can be a lot of fun. I'll show you just how easy it is to get started with an airbrush.

Structures, freight cars, and locomotives are just some of the things that can be painted with an airbrush. I'll share some basic painting techniques that will help you get started.

I may be a bit biased in saying airbrushing isn't difficult. My father was an auto body repairman with decades of painting experience, and I grew up watching him paint vehicles. Some of my early paint jobs didn't turn out that well, and I ruined a few models along the way. Instead of getting frustrated by mistakes, I kept airbrushing, asking questions, and adapting my techniques. It's been 20 years since I first picked up an airbrush, and I'm still learning new tips and tricks.

Selecting an airbrush

Choosing an airbrush that's right for you is a matter of personal preference, but you should select one that you can grip comfortably and easily reach the controls. Painting sessions take time, and they will seem much longer if you have an airbrush that isn't a good fit.

Some airbrushes are designed for certain types of work: either large-area coverage or fine work. Others can be fitted with different needles and nozzles for different applications.

Basically, there are two types of airbrushes: single-action and double-action. A single-action airbrush allows you to control the volume of air passing through the brush with the trigger, **1**. A double-action airbrush lets you regulate both the air and paint volumes with the trigger, **2**. The air on a double-action brush is controlled by pushing down on the spray button. The paint volume is adjusted by pulling back on the button. Double-action brushes are good for painting and weathering in tight areas where controlling paint volume is necessary.

Airbrushes are further categorized as external and internal mix. In external-mix airbrushes, the air and paint are mixed outside the airbrush. With an internal-mix airbrush, the air is drawn into the rear of the brush, while the paint is drawn, either by gravity or suction feed, into the middle.

External-mix airbrushes, which are all single-action, are good general-use brushes and easy to clean. Internal-mix brushes are better at atomizing paint into smaller particles but are more work to clean.

Some airbrushes are referred to as hybrids, 3. These are single-action brushes, but they mix the paint internally.

Air supply

Having a source of dry, clean compressed air is key for successful airbrushing. Air sources vary in type, price, and complexity. The cheapest is a propellant can. Though affordable, if you don't airbrush often, it's difficult to regulate the air flow from a can, and the can may freeze during extended painting sessions.

If you plan to airbrush on a more regular basis, an air compressor is a better long-term investment. Airbrush-specific compressors are priced between $100 and $400, depending on their features. Not all features are needed, but some, such as a pressure regulator, are useful. Small compressors are typically rated between 25 and 35 psi, ideal for most projects. However, for weathering, you don't need that much pressure, and the regulator will let you adjust the psi.

A moisture trap is another helpful feature. Humidity in a compressor can cause water droplets to pass through the airbrush and onto the model, ruining

CODY SAYS:

Never shake paint—always stir it. Shaking leaves paint around the top of the jar, where it dries into clumps that can clog an airbrush. Also, thinned paint dries in an open tip quickly. If you use a single-action brush, close it if it will sit for more than 20 seconds.

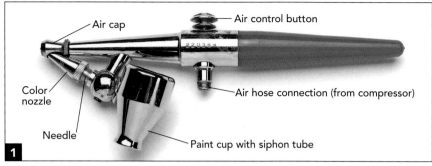

The Paasche H is an example of a single-action airbrush. With this style of brush, the air flow draws the paint up from the color cup (or bottle) into the angled paint nozzle. The knurled nozzle adjusts paint volume, and the button on the top controls the air flow.

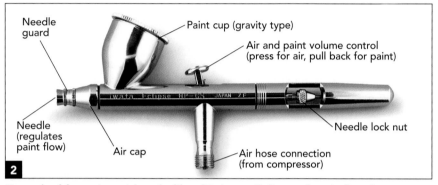

On a double-action airbrush, like this Iwata Eclipse, the air flow is controlled by pushing the trigger down, and the paint flow is controlled by pulling the button back. The paint flows into the body of the airbrush from a gravity-feed cup.

The Badger 200 is an example of a single-action airbrush with internal mixing. The brush has the longitudinal needle found on double-action brushes, but the paint volume is controlled by turning the knurled knob on the end of the needle instead of with the trigger.

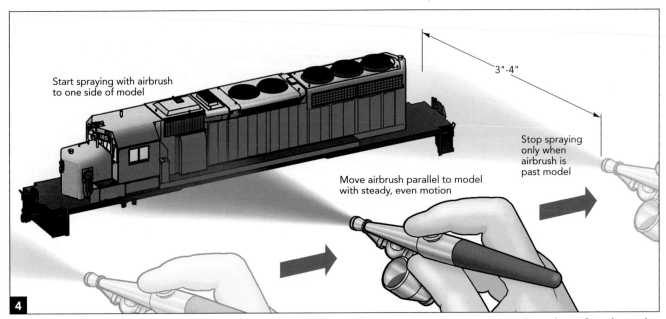

4

To achieve a smooth, even finish, move the airbrush as shown in this illustration. Overlap the edge of each stroke to get an even color across the model.

Start spraying with airbrush to one side of model

Move airbrush parallel to model with steady, even motion

Stop spraying only when airbrush is past model

3"-4"

the paint job. If you're unable to find a compressor with a moisture trap, you can splice a trap directly into the air hose. Moisture traps should be drained after each painting session.

About the only drawback to air compressors is that you can hear them running. Some compressors have an automatic shutoff feature to keep it from running when not in use. "Silent" models that use refrigerator-style compressors to charge small storage tanks are also available, but they're more expensive.

Types of paint

Once you have an airbrush and air source, the next thing you need is paint. The two types of paint used by model railroaders are acrylics, such as Testor's Model Master and Micro-Mark's MicroLux custom-blended hobby acrylics, among others, and organic-solvent-based, including Accu-paint and Scalecoat.

Organic-solvent-based paints have been used in the hobby for many years but must be handled with care. These paints may attack plastic, so you'll want to prime your models or apply a protective coating such as Scalecoat Shieldcoat. Also, organic-solvent-based paints must be used in a well-ventilated area, and you should wear a respirator, safety glasses, and nitrile rubber gloves.

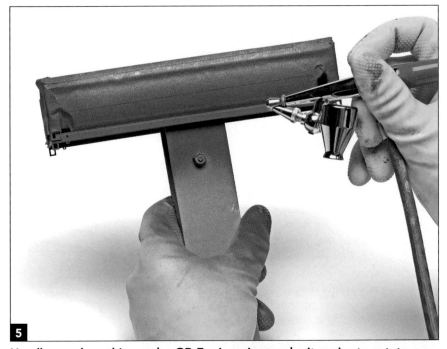

5

Handles, such as this one by GB Engineering, make it easier to rotate a model when airbrushing. You can also make your own handle from scrap wood or foam blocks, but use foam only with acrylic paints as organic-solvent-based paint will dissolve foam.

Safe for plastic, acrylic, or water-based, paints are available in the same range of colors as organic-solvent paints. Even though they're labeled as non-toxic, acrylics should still be used with caution (rubber gloves, respirator, and vented spray booth). Acrylics require a bit more air pressure (20-30 psi) than organic-solvent-based paints.

Acrylics and solvent-based paints are both sold ready for brush painting, which means you need to thin them for airbrushing. Start by stirring the paint thoroughly in the jar. It takes several minutes to remix a bottle of paint, particularly if it's been sitting on the shelf for a while. Tans, grays, and browns take the longest time to mix because

SOLVING COMMON PROBLEMS

Airbrushing problems are easy to solve, and many result from the variables involved: paint thinning, air pressure, and paint volume.

GRITTY PAINT: The finish looks like sandpaper, which is caused by paint particles drying before they reach the surface. Make sure the paint isn't too thin. Then lower the air pressure and hold the airbrush closer. Airbrushed paint should go on slightly wet.

NO PAINT COMES OUT: There is probably old paint in the nozzle that is preventing the paint from moving. You can use a cotton swab dipped in lacquer thinner to carefully remove dried paint.

OVERSPRAY: Watch where you're aiming. Make sure you mask any areas you don't want painted, or you may have to repaint them.

PAINT BLEEDS UNDER MASKING TAPE: This is usually caused by applying paint too heavily. Wet paint creeps under the tape to create a ragged line. Spray on several light coats instead of trying to cover with one heavy coat. Also, spray at an angle over the tape so the air pressure isn't forcing the paint under the tape.

RUNS: Too much paint. It builds up and runs down the surface. Try thinning the paint slightly, and/or use several thin coats instead of a single pass.

SPATTERS: Paint should leave the nozzle of the airbrush in an even, cone-shaped pattern. If the paint is uneven or if there are spatters of paint, the nozzle could be split, the tip of the needle bent, or both.

Move the needle's point across a fingertip, turning it slowly as you go. If it catches on your skin, then it's bent. To repair, drag the affected side across a medium grit sanding stick, test it, and repeat if necessary.

Check the nozzle with a magnifying glass, looking for a ragged tear at the opening. If the nozzle is damaged, you'll have to replace it.

SPIDERS: These paint spots with spreading, leg-like tendrils are caused by too much of everything: too much paint, too much thinner, spraying too close to the surface. Adjust the brush so only a small amount of paint comes out. Try spraying at reduced air pressure and if the paint is too thin add more paint to the mixture in the brush.

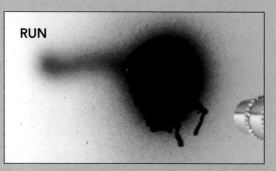
RUN

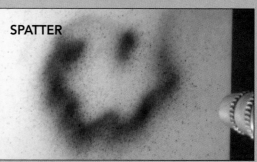
SPATTER

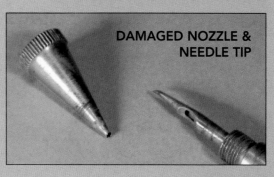
DAMAGED NOZZLE & NEEDLE TIP

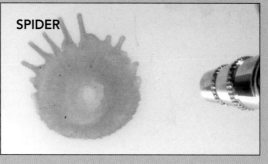
SPIDER

a large percentage of their pigment is clay. Keep stirring the paint until the pigment clumps are mixed completely with the liquid.

To make sure your paint is clean (and stays that way), never shake the jar. When shaken, paint gets onto the lip of the jar and dries into clumps. These clumps can fall into the paint and clog your airbrush. Putting a screen filter on the siphon tube will help keep clumps

out of the airbrush. Straining paint is an additional way to keep out foreign matter. Micro-Mark offers a strainer/funnel combination that's useful for this task.

After the paint is remixed, find a thinner that's clean (free of lint and dust) and compatible with the paint you're using. Any impurities in the thinner will get in your paint and on your model. Acrylic and organic-solvent-based thinners can't be used

interchangeably. In a separate jar, thin the paint until it reaches the consistency of milk. After your airbrushing session, empty the thinned paint into a waste-paint container. Never dump it back into the original jar.

Most manufacturers print the recommended thinner-to-paint ratio on the side of each jar, but consider that a starting point. Different colors (and bottles of paint) react differently. Thin

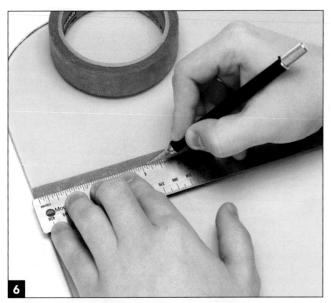

6 A favorite modeler's trick is to put masking tape on a piece of glass, lay a steel straightedge over it, and cut a strip using a hobby knife with a fresh no. 11 blade. Use the cut edge to mask the separation line between colors.

7 Even though the paint is dry, it can still peel off if you're not careful. Slowly pull the masking tape up and away at an acute angle from the last color applied. Don't leave the tape on the model too long, or it will leave residue on the model.

AIRBRUSH SUPPLIERS

Badger Air-Brush
badgerairbrush.com

Iwata Media
iwata-airbrush.com

Paasche Airbrush
paascheairbrush.com

Tamiya America
tamiyausa.com

Testor's Aztek
testors.com

the paint, spray it, and adjust as necessary. Weathering mixes must be thinned more than regular airbrush mixes. Pigments settle fast in paint thinned for weathering, so stir it regularly or add a few drops of flow enhancer.

Prep work and priming

Before you paint a model, clean it to remove any impurities that might affect paint adhesion or detract from the overall finish. The easiest way to clean a model is to wash it in warm, soapy water. I prefer Ivory liquid as it's almost pure soap and doesn't contain lotions. Keep an old toothbrush handy to clean any hard-to-reach areas.

After the model is clean, shake off the excess water, put it on a lint-free towel, and set it in a dust-free place such as a cabinet. Plastic, metal, and some resin models can be cleaned with this technique.

Commercial cleaners are also available for the various modeling mediums. Polly Scale manufactures Plastic Prep, an alcohol-based cleaner that removes mold release, silicone, and grease from plastic. Tarnished brass models can be cleaned with powdered copper cleaner, available at most grocery stores, and an old toothbrush.

With the prep work done, you should spray the model with an undercoat, which ensures that the final color or colors are even throughout the model. Light gray is a good, all-purpose undercoat color.

Painting and masking

Before you start spraying a model, test the paint on a similar material. This way, if the paint mix is too thin or not thinned enough, you won't ruin your model. Once you're satisfied with the paint flow, start spraying.

Hold the airbrush between 3" and 4" from the model and apply the paint with a smooth, even stroke, **4**. Start spraying beyond one end of the model, smoothly move the airbrush across the model, and stop spraying beyond the other end. Apply the paint in light coats, overlapping the edge of each stroke until the model is evenly covered. The paint should go on wet and shiny but dry quickly. If you apply the paint too heavily or don't let it dry completely between coats, it'll get thick and develop runs. If it goes on dry, you'll have a rough finish.

You may need to rotate the model while airbrushing to get paint into hard-to-reach areas, and that's where a paint handle proves helpful, **5**.

To gain experience with the airbrush, start with models that require only one color, such as a boxcar. When you feel more confident, try painting models with multiple colors. To prevent the second color from getting onto the first, the model will have to be masked. Regular 3M masking tape or the firm's blue painter's tape work well. However, masking tape doesn't have a perfectly straight edge, so you'll need to put a piece onto a pane of glass and cut it into strips using a new blade in a hobby knife or a single-edge blade, **6**. Use the freshly cut edge to mask the separation line. Make sure the tape is pressed down into grooves, over rivets and exterior posts, and in window openings.

Once the separation line is masked and the tape is snug, finish covering the model with full strips of tape. Then, to help keep the separation line crisp, lightly spray along the edge with the first color. After the paint has dried, apply the second color. Repeat the masking and painting process until all of the colors are applied.

You should give paint a full 24 hours to dry. When removing masking tape from a model, pull it up and away from the last color applied at a 45-degree angle to prevent the paint from lifting, **7**.

Safety first

No matter if you're using solvent-based paints or acrylics, paint fumes and particulates are harmful to your health. All painting should be done in a well-ventilated area, preferably a spray booth. Badger, North Coast Models, and Paasche, among others, produce spray booths that are ready for installation.

When you install a spray booth, keep it away from furnaces, water heaters, or other sources of ignition. Ideally, a spray booth should be vented to the outside air. If that can't be done, the Testor Corp. makes a spray booth that removes particles and filters air out the back. This booth should be used only with acrylic paints.

You can further protect yourself by wearing a respirator and nitrile rubber gloves (with organic-solvent paints) or latex gloves (with acrylic paints). The respirator will keep paint particles out of your lungs, and the gloves will keep paint off your hands.

The sky is the limit

After you've gained confidence painting models, you can weather them with an airbrush. It's a given that you'll have models that don't turn out well, but don't be discouraged. Learning how to airbrush well takes time, and the best way to learn is by practicing. In no time, you'll be painting models the way you want them to look, and you'll find out how much fun airbrushing can be.

CLEANING TIPS

When I first started airbrushing, my father told me, "If you treat your airbrush well, it'll treat you well." Nothing could be truer. With proper handling and cleaning, it should last you many years, but if you don't clean and maintain your airbrush, your painting sessions won't be enjoyable (and your models won't look that good, either). You should follow the manufacturer's cleaning instructions, but here are a few other pointers to follow to keep your airbrush operating its best:

- Never store your brush with paint (or cleaner) in it.
- Disassemble and clean your brush after each painting session.
- If you're only changing colors, you can just rinse the brush unless you're going from a dark color to a light one.
- Keep rinsing until the cleaning solution comes out clear.
- Enamel and acrylics take different solvents and cleaners (enamels: mineral spirits and lacquer thinner, acrylics: distilled water and Windex).
- After reassembling the brush, reconnect it to an air supply and blow a little lacquer thinner through it to make sure nothing remains.
- If you use a double-action or hybrid brush, oil the needle before storing.

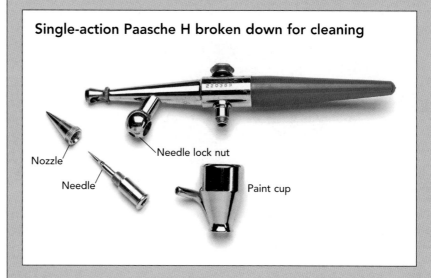

Single-action Paasche H broken down for cleaning

Nozzle

Needle

Needle lock nut

Paint cup

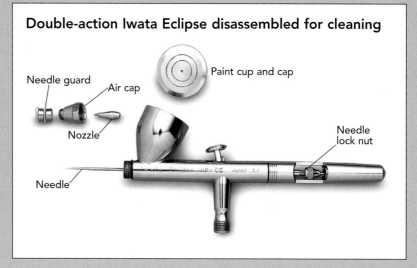

Double-action Iwata Eclipse disassembled for cleaning

Needle guard

Air cap

Nozzle

Paint cup and cap

Needle

Needle lock nut

Loosen paint jar caps

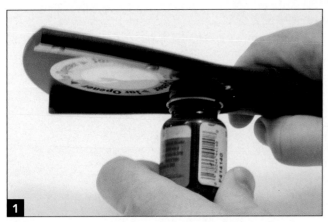

1 The Oxo jar opener has metal teeth which makes it easy to remove stuck paint jar caps. Use these with care, though, as the teeth can rip metal caps.

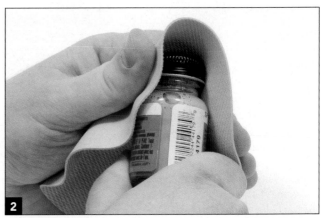

2 A rubber jar grabber, often available for free at county fairs and home shows, is a cheaper solution for loosening caps. It also does a good job of protecting your hands when opening paint bottles.

3 While more commonly used in automotive and plumbing repair, a strap wrench can also be used to remove a stuck paint bottle cap.

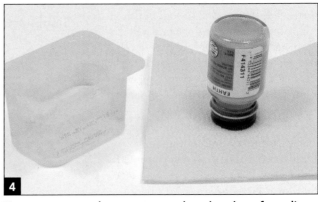

4 Tap water can release caps stuck to bottles of acrylic paint. Let the bottle stand upside down with water in the cap for 5–10 minutes, and it should pop right off.

If you've done painting for any amount of time, you've undoubtedly encountered a stubborn paint bottle cap. You know the ones. You twist and twist until your hands turn red, hoping that cap will budge. I used to use pliers to solve this problem, but they often damaged the cap, and one time I even broke the bottle! I have found four techniques for removing paint bottle caps that require far less effort.

In the spray booth at *Model Railroader*, we use an Oxo Good Grips jar opener (no. 21191) to open stubborn paint bottle caps. These are sold at most major discount stores and specialty cooking shops. Just place the cap into the bottom of the opener and rotate counterclockwise, **1**. I've found it best to apply light to moderate pressure as the metal teeth can rip the cap.

Another kitchen gadget that works well is a rubber jar grabber, **2**. These are sold at the same places as the Oxo tool, or you can get them for free at county fairs or home shows. (Just look around the exhibition hall—that's where I found mine.) The grabber is fairly reliable, and it saves a lot of wear and tear on your hands.

A third option is a strap wrench. I found mine in the "As seen on TV" section of a local drug store several years ago, and I've seen similar products at hardware stores and auto supply centers. The wrench features a plastic handle with a rubber strap. After fitting the strap around the lid, twist the wrench counterclockwise until the cap pops off, **3**.

The final fix is warm tap water. That's right. If you use acrylic paints, hold the bottle upside down and dunk the cap in warm water, **4**. Let the bottle stand on end for 5–10 minutes, and twist the cap. You may want to use the rubberized jar grabber or strap wrench in conjunction with this technique.

If you do any painting, keep these techniques in mind. Your wrists and hands will thank you, and you'll have more time to spend modeling.

Airbrush models with acrylic paint

These days it seems like acrylic paints have always been a part of the hobby, but they've been commonly available only since the 1990s. Before then, the only decisions we had to make when painting a model were what brand we wanted to use and whether we wanted enamel or lacquer. But in the short time acrylics have been around, they've gained popularity with modelers and are now offered in many of the same colors as enamels and lacquers.

What makes the three types of paint different? Acrylics, enamels, and lacquers all vary in chemical composition, which determines how they dry. Acrylics dry by the evaporation of water (they're water-based, remember). Lacquers also dry by evaporation, but in this case it's their solvents that evaporate. Enamels (both water- and solvent-based) rely on auto-oxidation, or contact with oxygen in the air, to dry.

Acrylics work just as well as other types of paints but require some different techniques. Follow along as I

You can finish locomotives, freight cars, and structures with acrylic paints, whether you spray it on or use a brush. These water-based paints offer a variety of benefits.

describe some of the basics of working with acrylics. Before long, you'll be painting locomotives, freight cars, and structures with these water-based paints.

What's in paint?

Acrylic paint is often referred to as water-based. Though not incorrect, there is much more to acrylic paint than just pigment and water. In fact, there are four primary ingredients in paint: pigment, resin, solvents, and additives.

The pigment gives the paint its color and opacity. The paint film, which we see on our models, is formed by the resin (sometimes referred to as the binder). Manufacturers then add a solvent (or thinner) to dilute the paint and control its drying rate and flow characteristics, among other things. The last ingredients are the additives, such as fillers and driers, that further

adjust a paint's properties.

For more information on paint chemistry, visit the Testor Corp. website (testors.com). Click on Hobbyist Guides in the blue bar near the top of the page, and then click on the link Understanding Paint.

Why acrylics?

Acrylic paint is popular with modelers for many reasons, primarily safety. Acrylics don't contain the harmful solvents used in organic, solvent-based paints. However, acrylics should still be used with care, as covered in "Safety precautions" on page 83.

Another reason to use acrylics is that they don't attack plastic. The solvents used in enamels and lacquers can craze plastic, especially if a primer or protective coating isn't applied, **1**. Acrylics have a milder chemical composition, making them plastic compatible.

1

One of the advantages of acrylic paint is that it doesn't attack plastic. The shell on this locomotive crazed (wrinkled) when it was sprayed with organic-solvent-based lacquer.

2

Dried paint and pigment clumps can clog an airbrush or ruin the finish on a model. This filter, sold by Micro-Mark, attaches to the siphon tube and keeps contaminants out of the paint stream.

Finally, acrylics dry quickly and can be covered with solvent-based finishes such as Testor's Dullcote and Glosscote. (They can also be sprayed with special acrylic clears, such as those produced by Polly Scale and Microscale.) Enamels resist chemicals, but they take several days to fully cure and lacquers can react to certain solvents.

Badger Air-Brush Co., the Testor Corp., and Tamiya, among others, all offer acrylic paints. Badger's Modelflex and Railflyer Model Prototypes are produced in an assortment of railroad colors, while Tamiya's paint line is geared toward military modelers. However, Tamiya offers many general colors (black, red, green, etc.) that have model railroad applications, and other colors in its line can be easily mixed.

Stirred, not shaken

The pathway to a successful finish with acrylics starts with mixing the paint thoroughly. Paints contain pigments that settle to the bottom of the jar. These pigments need to be completely mixed into the liquid before painting.

Though tempting, never shake a jar of paint. The paint will dry on the lip of the jar and turn into clumps that will contaminate the clean paint. I always attach a filter to the siphon tube when airbrushing to prevent impurities

from clogging the airbrush, **2**.

Once the paint is remixed, you're ready to begin brush-painting. But if you're going to airbrush acrylics, you still need to thin the paint.

Airbrushing with acrylics

Badger, the Testor Corp., and Tamiya all have thinner for their respective lines of acrylics. Some modelers prefer thinning paints with distilled water or 70 percent isopropyl alcohol, but it's best to use the thinner designed for the paint you're using to avoid any mishaps.

Most manufacturers print the paint-to-thinner ratios on the label, but you should use those as a starting point only. Certain paints require more thinning than others, so start with the recommended amount of thinner, test the mix, and keep thinning until you have an even spray pattern. I've found that thinning the paint to the consistency of milk works best.

When spraying acrylics, use the largest nozzle produced for your airbrush. Acrylics dry fast and smaller nozzles tend to clog up with paint. It's also good practice to keep a cotton swab and cup of warm water near your spray booth to clean dry paint off the nozzle.

Once you've finished using your airbrush, dump the unused paint into

a waste container. Air and thinner cause the paint to break down, so never dump paint back into the original jar.

Also, be sure to clean your airbrush immediately after each painting session. Disassemble the airbrush, soak the parts in warm water, and clean the components with cotton swabs and pipe cleaners. Any stubborn paint can be removed with Windex window cleaner or paint remover designed specifically for acrylics.

Problems and solutions

Newcomers and even long-time users of acrylics have bad painting sessions periodically. The number of problems that can crop up when airbrushing are great, but I'll highlight three.

CODY SAYS:

Airbrushing with acrylics is a skill that takes time to learn. Start with simple projects to gain confidence and go from there. There will be projects that don't turn out as you'd hoped, but that's part of the process. The best way to grow your skills is to keep airbrushing.

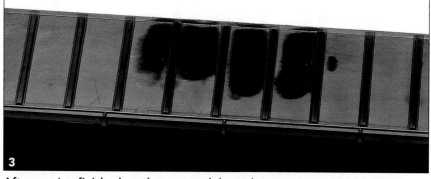

3

After you've finished work on a model, wash it in warm, soapy water to clean off any impurities. Greasy fingerprints and mold release causes acrylic paint to bead up and be repelled from the model.

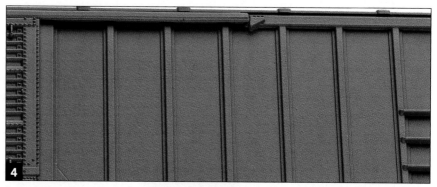

4

Rough finishes not only look bad, but they make it difficult to add decals. During painting, the airbrush was held too far away from this boxcar, causing the paint to dry before it hit the model.

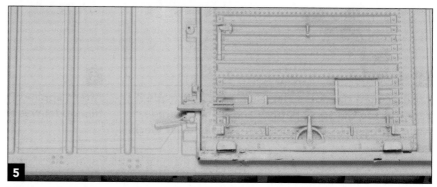

5

When airbrushing acrylic paints, build up the color in light layers. If the paint is applied too thick, it will pool around details and cause the model to have an uneven sheen.

Many first-time airbrush users experience problems with paint beading up or repelling from the model's surface. This is caused by impurities, such as skin oils, or mold release, **3**. Washing the model in warm water with a few drops of liquid dish detergent will remove most impurities. Commercial model cleaners, such as Testor's Plastic Prep, also work well.

Rough finishes, as shown in photo **4**, can be traced to one (or more) of three things: the air pressure is set too high, the airbrush is too far from the model, or there's not sufficient paint passing through the nozzle. Holding the airbrush 3" to 4" from the model and setting the air pressure at 20 to 30 psi is sufficient for acrylics.

Photo **5** shows that paint can also be applied too heavily. This is caused by thinning the paint too much, not moving the airbrush across the model surface fast enough, or holding the airbrush too close to the model. When airbrushing, the goal is to move the airbrush parallel to the model in a smooth motion.

Get painting
Acrylic paints have properties that are different from those of lacquers or enamels, but once you've worked with them for a while, you'll find them easy to use.

If you'd like more information on acrylics, read Jeff Wilson's book *Basic Painting and Weathering for Model Railroaders, Second Edition* (Kalmbach, 2014). For now, though, get the colors you need and an unpainted model, and enjoy the fun of painting with acrylics.

Paint yellow boxcars

1

Painting yellow freight cars, such as this Athearn HO scale Railbox boxcar, can be difficult. But with a few tricks used by veteran modelers, you can get yellow to cover easily and evenly.

2

An even coat of Polly Scale Flat Aluminum ensures the yellow will cover evenly in just two or three coats. Fewer coats of paint makes it easier to preserve the model's fine details.

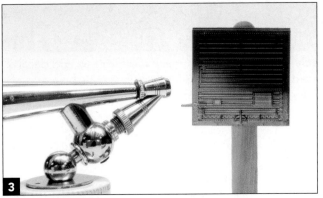

3

I also painted the doors Flat Aluminum. This made it easier to see the spray pattern and paint coverage while I airbrushed the doors with Steam Power Black.

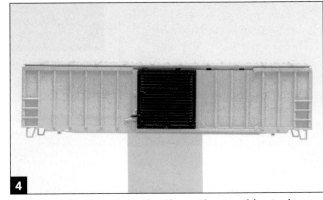

4

After I applied Polly Scale Clear Gloss and let it dry, the model was ready for decals and weathering.

Several years ago, I purchased some undecorated Athearn 50-foot Railbox boxcar kits at a local hobby shop. Wanting to add some variety to my rolling stock fleet, I decided to model the cars in Railbox colors but with Burlington Northern reporting marks, **1**. Easy enough, right? Well, not so fast. As most veteran modelers know, yellow is a difficult color to apply. But with a few tricks, you can apply yellow (and any other bright color) like a professional.

Before painting any model, it's important to wash it in warm water with a few drops of dish soap added. This removes oils and other impuri-ties that might affect paint adhesion. After cleaning it, I let the model air dry on a lint-free towel. For the dura-tion of the project, I only handled the model while wearing powder-free latex gloves.

Once the model was dry, I sprayed the body shell, doors, and brake wheel with an even coat of Polly Scale Flat Aluminum. This serves two purposes. First, it helps ensure the final colors will cover evenly. Second, the silver makes it easier to apply the yellow in two or three coats, **2**. It would take many coats of yellow to cover the unpainted black plastic shell, increasing the risk of runs and ponding, among other problems.

You're probably wondering why I painted the doors silver, since they're black to start with. If you've ever tried spraying black paint on black plas-tic, you know it's difficult to see how the paint is covering. With the doors painted silver, it's much easier to see the spray pattern and coverage, **3**.

I let the yellow and black paint dry thoroughly (at least 24 hours, or until there is no discernible odor) before spraying the car with Polly Scale Clear Gloss, **4**. Then I decaled the car and weathered it using techniques covered on page 107. Once I installed the trucks and couplers, the car was ready for revenue service.

Tint turn signals and taillights

1 I first painted the green taillights silver. This is the key to making the taillights translucent.

2 A round-head toothpick makes a handy applicator for the tinted Kristal Klear. Though it looks opaque at this point, it will dry translucent.

3 I added two drops of yellow food coloring to the red-tinted Kristal Klear for the front (orange) turn signals.

4 The grill on this model also features Chevy's trademark Bowtie. I used yellow-tinted Kristal Klear to fill in the ornament.

The number of vehicle models available today is greater than ever. Though the selection of makes and models is large, it's the small things that make or break scale models of cars and trucks. Take for example, this custom-decorated HO scale Burlington Northern pickup. The model is painted green; has the BN herald, name, and vehicle number on the door; and the vehicle weight is shown on the box. But upon closer examination, you'll notice the taillights, turn signals, and Chevy Bowtie are unpainted. But with Microscale Kristal Klear and food coloring, I made translucent turn signals and an authentic looking grill ornament.

I started by working on the taillights. I used a silver paint marker to color the taillights silver, **1**. This is the key to making the taillights translucent. The paint is fast drying, but I let it set for 30 minutes before proceeding.

Next, I poured a small puddle of Microscale Kristal Klear onto a scrap piece of styrene. Don't work on paper as the Kristal Klear and food coloring will soak through it. Then I added one drop of red food coloring and mixed it into the Kristal Klear with a toothpick. It takes about 30 seconds to get the food coloring stirred in evenly.

Then I used a round-head toothpick to apply the red-tinted Kristal Klear, **2**. If you don't like how an application looks, simply wipe it off. Kristal Klear is water soluble.

To make the orange for the front turn signals, I added two drops of yellow food coloring into the red-tinted Kristal Kleer (as we learned in grade school, red and yellow makes orange). Since the front grill is plated plastic designed to simulate chrome, I didn't have to paint the turn signals silver beforehand. I used another toothpick to apply the orange-tinted Kristal Klear, **3**.

Finally, I poured a pushpin-head size puddle of Kristal Klear onto the styrene and tinted it with yellow food coloring. I also used this to color the Chevy Bowtie, **4**.

Enhancing the realism of a vehicle model is quick and easy with this technique. Just check with your wife first before you raid her stash of food coloring!

Detail with different brands of decals

I used decals from Rail Graphics and Microscale to letter this Atlas HO scale General Electric Dash 8-40B diesel locomotive. Though both companies use water-slide decals, they each required slightly different preparation before application.

When modeling a free-lanced railroad like the HO scale Milwaukee, Racine & Troy, you often have to letter the equipment using decals from different sets and manufacturers. This was the case with MR&T General Electric Dash 8-40B no. 1100, **1**. I used a custom-produced set of Rail Graphics decals for the railroad herald and end stripes, and assorted Microscale sets for the balance of the unit. Though both firms produce water-slide decals, the preparation work is a bit different for each brand.

Rail Graphics decals are printed on a solid sheet of decal film, while Microscale spot-prints film around each graphic, **2**. I cut as close as possible to the MR&T herald (and also the end stripes) to eliminate excess film, **3**. I cut the decals on a piece of plate glass so I didn't tear the decal or get jagged edges.

After cutting each decal from the carrier sheet, I soaked it in distilled water for 10–20 seconds (or until it slid freely from the backing paper), **4**. Though regular tap water will work, it often has minerals in it that may dry as white spots on the finished model.

While each decal was soaking, I applied Microscale Micro Set to the area where it would be set. I carefully positioned each decal with a toothpick. Then I blotted the excess water and pushed out air bubbles with a cosmetic sponge, **5**. This helps the decal conform to uneven surfaces, such as battery box doors.

I let the decals dry overnight before applying Microscale Micro Sol setting solution. This product softens the decals so they conform to irregular surfaces on the model, such as nut-bolt-washer castings for the grab irons and the spaces between the doors on the hood. Let the Micro Sol dry completely before touching the decals, as

they can easily be damaged during this step.

After applying the Micro Sol, I noticed that there were several air bubbles under the decal film for the end stripes. I used a sharp no. 11 blade to poke the air bubbles, **6**. Apply gentle pressure to the blade so you don't gouge the plastic.

With the air bubbles popped, I applied a second application of Micro Sol with a Microbrush, **7**. I repeated this process until all the air bubbles were gone. Take your time and be diligent about removing the bubbles. Any that you miss will show up as silver-looking blotches under clear flat or satin finishes, which doesn't look realistic.

As nice as it is to have all of the decals for your model in one set, that isn't always possible. Examine each set of decals and follow the manufacturer's directions. In the end, you'll be rewarded with a good looking model.

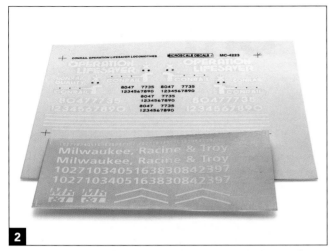

2

Rail Graphics decals are printed on a solid sheet of decal film, while Mircroscale spot-prints film around the graphics.

3

I used a straightedge and a fresh no. 11 blade to cut the MR&T herald from the Rail Graphics decal sheet. I did the cutting on a piece of plate glass so I wouldn't tear the decal.

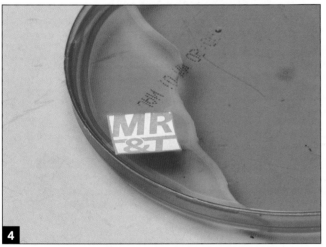

4

To prevent minerals from drying as white spots on the model, soak the decals in distilled water for 10–20 seconds or until they slide off the carrier sheet easily.

5

After positioning the decal, use a cosmetic sponge to blot away excess water and push out any trapped air bubbles.

6

Uh-oh! After the Micro Sol dried, I noticed air bubbles under the end stripes. I carefully popped the bubbles using a sharp no. 11 blade.

7

A second application of Micro Sol eliminated more of the bubbles. Repeat this process until there are no more bubbles visible.

Model patch out freight cars

Weathered freight cars with restenciled reporting marks add realism to your rolling stock.

I f you've sat at a grade crossing recently, you've probably noticed freight cars and locomotives with the original reporting marks painted over and new ones applied. On the prototype, this is done because the equipment's ownership has changed. Modeling cars with restenciled reporting marks is a quick and easy way to add realism to your modern-era layout. Here, I'll show you two easy ways to restencil, or "patch out," reporting marks on your rolling stock.

The first technique requires a simple-to-build styrene mask. Making a styrene mask is a simple one-evening project, and you can use it multiple times. The second technique uses a solid-color decal sheet, called trim film, to cover the reporting marks. Trim film has the same properties as regular decals, and is available in a

variety of colors. Though the models shown here are HO, you can easily adapt these techniques to any other scale.

Don't just limit yourself to freight cars. Locomotives operated by Union Pacific and BNSF Ry., as well as numerous short line and regional railroads, have their original markings covered and new ones applied. This is cheaper than repainting the entire unit.

The inspiration for my restenciling projects comes from photographs that I've taken while railfanning. Also, websites such as railcarphotos.com and locophotos.com have extensive photo collections that are searchable by reporting mark.

Making a mask
I needed to restencil a dozen Walthers HO scale Clinchfield quad-hopper kits with the BGSX (Strata Corp.) reporting mark for use on my Minnesota Northern RR layout. Masking exterior-post cars with tape can be tricky as well as time consuming. An easier and quicker way to patch out the original reporting marks is to use a homemade styrene mask and an airbrush.

To match the sequence of the prototype, I weathered the cars before patching out the reporting marks, **1**. I weathered the Clinchfield hoppers, which were originally used to haul coal but now carry aggregates, with thinned Polly Scale Reefer White,

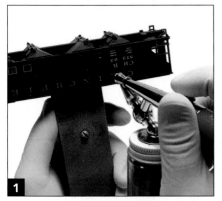

1 I weathered the Clinchfield hoppers with thinned Polly Scale Reefer White, Dirt, and Steam Power Black before patching out the reporting marks.

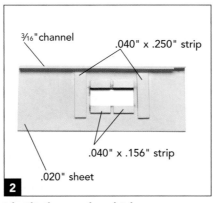

2 I built the mask, which covers about half of the hopper, out of pieces of styrene.

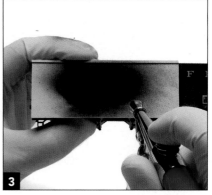

3 Set the air compressor at 20–25 psi, and apply the paint carefully in multiple layers, so it doesn't seep under the mask.

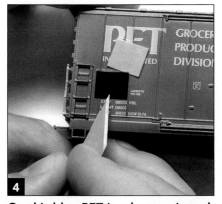

4 On this blue PET Inc. boxcar, I used black patches from a Tangent Scale Models decal set as a background for the restenciled white numbers and letters.

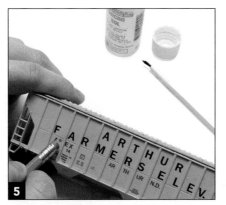

5 To remove the original lettering on a car when using a light-colored trim film, brush Micro Sol over the lettering and use a pencil eraser to take off the lettering.

6 For crisp square edges on your trim film, cut it with a cutting tool having a fresh blade.

Steam Power Black. I mixed my weathering colors at 10–30 drops of paint to a ½ ounce of 70 percent isopropyl alcohol. As you go, build up the paint in multiple layers. Work slowly and check your progress between coats, since it's easy to weather a car too heavily.

Next, I built the mask using styrene, **2**. The mask covers about half of the car, which is sufficient as long as you apply the paint carefully, **3**. Set the air compressor at 20 to 25 psi, and apply the paint in multiple layers. If you put the paint on too thick, it will seep under the mask.

Once I'd painted over the original reporting marks, I sprayed the car with Polly Scale Clear Gloss, as decals adhere best to a smooth, glossy surface.

Trim film patches

A second option for restenciling freight cars is to use trim film. Microscale offers the film in more than 20 colors, so finding a color to match your project shouldn't be too difficult.

On a blue PET Inc. boxcar, I used black patches from a Tangent Scale Models decal set that was designed to restencil its HO scale PS-2CD 4,000-cubic-foot-capacity covered hopper, **4**.

If you're using a light-colored trim film, such as yellow or white, it's a good idea to remove the original lettering on the car so it doesn't show through, **5**. To do this on a yellow hopper, I first brushed Micro Sol over the lettering. Then, with the Micro Sol still wet, I used a pencil eraser to remove the lettering. Don't use too

much pressure, or you'll remove the paint. I repeated this process until the lettering was gone.

Prototype restenciling is often done in a hurry and can come out pretty sloppy, so don't worry if your cuts aren't perfect. However, if you want the trim film to have nice, square edges, cut it with a cutting tool such as NorthWest Short Line's Chopper II, **6**. Be sure to keep a fresh blade in the Chopper, otherwise the edges of the trim film will be ragged and splinter apart when soaked in water.

Decaling and lettering

The final step in restenciling the cars is to add the new reporting marks using number and letter decals. I'm not a big fan of cutting individual numbers and letters directly from a decal sheet because it's too easy to damage adjacent

7 To cut out decals for new reporting marks, use a scissors to cut out a row of numbers and letters and then cut out what you need with a razor blade.

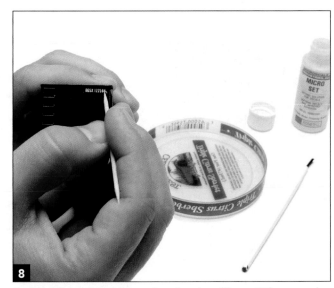

8 Apply Micro Set where the decals will go. When ready, slide the decals off the backing paper and position them on the model with a toothpick.

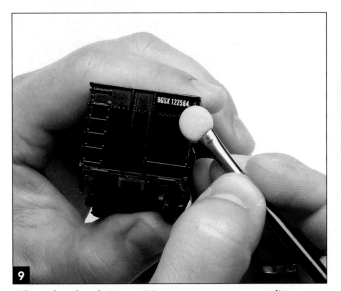

9 When the decals in position, use a sponge applicator to blot away excess water instead of cotton swabs or paper towels, which can leave lint on the model.

10 Allow the new reporting marks to dry overnight and then apply Micro Sol with a paintbrush to soften the decal and let it settle into the details of the car.

decals. Instead, I use scissors to cut out a row of numbers and letters. Then, I use a single-edge razor blade to cut out what I need, **7**. Do this on a hard surface, such as plate glass. To minimize the amount of decal film that will be visible, cut as close to the letters and numbers as possible.

I then soaked the decals in distilled water, which unlike tap water is free of minerals that can dry as white spots.

While the decal was soaking, I used a paintbrush to apply Micro Set to the area I was working on. Once the decals slid freely off the backing paper, I set

them on the model and carefully positioned them with a toothpick, **8**.

With the decals positioned, I used a sponge applicator, available from Micro-Mark, to blot away the excess water, **9**. Though cotton swabs and paper towels would also work, I don't recommend using them. Lint and fibers from these items can wind up on the model. Trying to pull fibers out from under a decal without damaging it isn't much fun. Don't ask me how I know this.

I let the new reporting marks dry overnight, and then I used a paintbrush to apply Micro Sol, **10**. The Micro Sol

softened the decal, so it would settle down into the carbody details. Let the Micro Sol dry completely before touching the decals.

After a few hours, I came back with a sharp hobby knife, poked trapped air bubbles, and applied more Micro Sol. I repeated this process as needed.

Next, I carefully wiped the model with a damp sponge to remove impurities and let it dry before using an airbrush to apply Polly Scale Clear Flat. The flat finish protects the decals, hides any remaining film, and gives the model a realistic appearance.

WEATHERING

Enhancing the appearance of locomotives, freight cars, and structures can be accomplished with weathering. In this section, I'm going to share a variety of techniques, including tried-and-true methods such as using powdered pastels, washes, and drybrushing, as well as newer techniques like artist's oils and makeup applicators.

Which technique is best? That's really a matter of personal preference. In some cases, one method isn't enough—I sometimes combine two, three, or more types of weathering to get the results I'm after. On the BNSF Ry. SW1000 shown above, I used makeup applicators to apply the rust effects on top of the cab and hood, airbrushed the knuckle couplers using a simple three-step process, and applied a wash made from artist's oils.

It wasn't all that long ago that I was reluctant to weather my models, but now I find it very rewarding. If you want to make your locomotives, freight cars, and structures look prototypical, give weathering a try.

Weather and string line poles

1 Weathered line poles add realism along a railroad's right-of-way, as shown here on *Model Railroader*'s Milwaukee, Racine & Troy railroad.

No matter what era you model, line poles can enhance the realism of your model railroad, **1**. For decades, line poles were a common sight along the railroad right-of-way. Though most are no longer in service, line poles can still be found trackside today, **2**.

From the 1800s until the 1960s, you could find line poles strung with communication and power lines along railroad rights-of-way.

Mainline poles, as seen in photo 2, might have three, four, or even five arms filled with wires. A barely used branch line might have poles with just two wires attached to insulators on brackets. The most common configuration was a line pole having one or more 10-pin crossarms, with five pins on each side of the pole, **3**. This is the type of pole I modeled for the MR&T, as seen in photo 1. These poles carried telephone and telegraph wires as well as power lines for railroad equipment such as lineside signals and switch machines.

Modeling line poles

Modeling and installing line poles is easy. Commercial poles are available in HO, N, and O scales, although you could also make your own using dowels and stripwood. Painting and weathering the poles can be done with a few basic colors, and clear-tint paints from Tamiya make simulating insulators a snap. Installing overhead wires can turn a simple pole line into an attention getter on your layout.

There are a variety of sources for HO scale line poles, including Bachmann, Rix Products, and Atlas Model Railroad Co, **4**. In addition, Rapido Trains makes Totally Wired telephone poles, which come factory wired and ready to install. Walthers sells electric utility pole kits, and Scale Structures Limited offers crossarms, insulators, and brackets.

The pool of products in N and O scales is smaller. Line poles are offered in N scale by Atlas and Bachmann, and crossarms are produced by Depots by John. In O scale, poles are manufactured by Weaver Scale Models.

2 Line poles were prominent along rights-of-way since the 1800s, and they can still be found along some tracks, such as the Union Pacific's main line through Nebraska in 2006.

3 On this branch line of the Pennsylvania RR, the line poles were configured with single 10-pin crossarms.

4 Poles in HO scale are available from a variety of manufacturers including Bachmann, Rix, and Atlas. I selected the Rix poles to use on the MR&T.

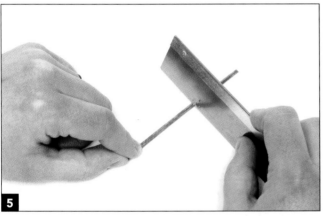

5 The plastic poles have molded wood grain detail, but to give them more of a rough texture, I scraped the poles with a fine-tooth razor saw.

6 After scraping the poles, they had a more realistic look, but this technique left plastic shavings on the poles. I removed the shavings with a scuff pad, and then washed the poles in warm, soapy water to remove plastic residue from the wood grain.

I selected the Rix Products railroad telephone poles for this project. Though the plastic poles have molded wood grain detail, it doesn't stand out that much. To give the poles a realistically rough texture, I scraped them with a fine-tooth razor saw (having 42 teeth per inch), **5**.

One drawback of using this technique is the leftover plastic shavings on the poles, so I removed the shavings with a scuff pad, **6**. I also rinsed the poles in warm, soapy water to clean the plastic residue out of the wood grain. I let the poles air dry and then attached the crossarms with liquid plastic cement.

I wanted the poles along the right-of-way to look like they'd been in place for a while, so I painted them grayish-brown, **7**. To achieve this look, I first applied a ring of full-strength Polly Scale Earth at the base of the pole. With the paint still wet, I used a Microbrush soaked in water to pull the paint toward the top of the pole, in effect creating a wash. It's okay if the molded brown plastic shows through Earth paint.

After the Earth paint had dried, I used the same techniques, but with L&N Gray, to give the poles a faded, sun-bleached look, **8**. I applied only one coat of gray, but more could be added if you want the poles to look even older. Once the gray dried, I painted the crossarm brackets with Polly Scale Tarnished Black.

Most telephone and telegraph insulators were made of clear or green glass. To complete the poles, I painted the insulators using a two-step process. First, I used a fine Microbrush to paint each insulator with Tamiya XF-16 Flat Aluminum, **9**. Then, I used a second Microbrush to apply the same firm's X-25 Clear Green, **10**.

Installing the line poles

Prototype line poles are spaced anywhere from 100 to 150 feet apart, so you may want to apply selective compression. Many modelers space the poles on 12" centers in HO scale, and 6" in N scale. I set the poles on the MR&T 25 scale feet from the track centerline, **11**. Depending on the width of the right of way, the poles should be at least 13 feet from the nearest rail.

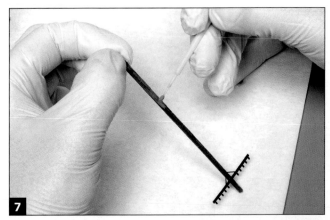

7 To give the textured poles a weathered look, I painted them grayish-brown, starting with a coat of Polly Scale Earth.

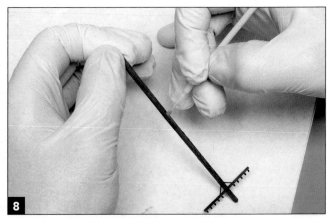

8 I followed the Earth with a coat of L&N Gray to complete the sun-bleached look. I also painted the crossarm brackets Polly Scale Tarnished Black.

9 I painted the insulators using a two-step process. I first painted the insulators with Tamiya XF-16 Flat Aluminum.

10 For the second step, I brushed on Tamiya X-25 Clear Green. This re-creates the look of prototype glass insulators.

11 I selectively compressed the spacing of the poles and set them 25 scale feet from the track's centerline. Prototype line poles are spaced anywhere from 100 to 150 feet apart.

12 I applied CA to the insulators and held the Pro Line Pole Line in position until it dried.

Stringing wires is an optional step, but it definitely enhances the realism of the line poles. I used Pro Line Pole Line from Pro Tech (protechmodelparts. com). This elastic polymer thread holds its shape even if it's bumped.

I started by applying quick-setting cyanoacrylate adhesive (CA) to the side of an insulator, **12**. Then I set the line in the adhesive and held it for 10 seconds, which is enough time for the glue to set. I repeated this process on insulators in the same position on subsequent poles until the line was strung.

Create hard-working diesel locomotives

1

Alco locomotives were known for belching black exhaust, and that grimy look really stands out on a bright yellow locomotive.

Diesel locomotives are hard-working machines. From the instant they roll out of the factory, they begin accumulating dirt, dust, grease, and grime. Though this makes prototype locomotives look less than pristine, it gives us inspiration for weathering our scale models.

When I was looking for a locomotive to weather for this project, I came across the HO scale Burlington Northern Alco C-425 (an Atlas Spokane, Portland & Seattle model that I renumbered for BN), **1**. Alco locomotives were notorious for belching oily, black exhaust, and that grimy look really pops on a bright yellow locomotive.

When weathering a locomotive, I like to combine different weathering techniques and media. I airbrushed and drybrushed Polly Scale acrylic paints, and applied a wash of Burnt Sienna oil paint with a brush. By combining various techniques and paints, I was able to create a more realistic locomotive.

I find that the best weathering results are achieved when working from prototype photos. There are numerous books, magazines, and websites that have color photos of diesels. Railroad historical societies might also be able to help you find images of a specific engine.

If you want to turn your shiny plastic or brass diesel locomotives into realistically weathered models that look like they work hard to earn their keep, give these techniques a try.

Weathering wheels

Though most of today's locomotive models come with blackened-metal wheels, they're far too shiny and the color is wrong. New wheelsets may be gray for a brief time, but they quickly become rusty and begin to accumulate dirt, dust, and grease.

To make the wheels more realistic, I first clean the faces with a cotton swab dipped in 70 percent isopropyl alcohol. This removes any impurities that will

affect paint adhesion. Then I apply Polly Scale Railroad Tie Brown with a Microbrush, being careful to keep paint off the electrical contacts, **2**. Don't worry if paint gets on the wheel treads. This can be cleaned off with a cotton swab dipped in Windex.

Truck sideframes

Fortunately, the truck sideframes on this model were removable, which made weathering much simpler. As with the wheels, I cleaned the sideframes with isopropyl alcohol to remove any oil and grease.

After the alcohol evaporated, I airbrushed the sideframes with thinned Polly Scale Dirt. Then I brush-painted the moving parts of the trucks, such as the springs and brake shoes, with the same firm's Rust, **3**. I thinned the paint with water so it wouldn't be opaque.

I finished weathering the trucks by doing some reverse weathering, **4**. The Railroad Tie Brown looked too

2 To make wheels appear rusty, I applied Polly Scale Railroad Tie Brown with a Microbrush.

Springs   Brake shoe

3 After airbrushing the sideframes, I brush-painted the moving parts of the trucks a rust color.

4 I finished weathering the trucks by drybrushing black on the face of each sideframe to show slivers of clean black paint.

5 Slide a wheel mask between the truck sideframes and the wheels to prevent a shadowing effect on the wheel faces.

uniform for my taste, so I drybrushed Engine Black on the face of each sideframe to represent slivers of clean black paint, just as I'd seen in prototype photos. It's important to pull the brush straight down on each stroke, otherwise you'll end up with wavy and unrealistic streaks of paint.

If the sideframes on your locomotive cannot be removed, you can use wheel masks, such as those from Summit Customcuts, to prevent a "shadowing" effect from appearing on the wheel faces. The styrene mask slips between the truck sideframes and the wheels, **5**. It is designed for modern six-axle locomotives made by Athearn (Ready-to-Roll and Genesis lines), Atlas, Broadway Limited, and Kato.

Another option is to attach electrical leads to the motor to keep the wheels in motion while you're airbrushing.

Fuel tank

The fuel tank is at truck level, so I weathered it with Dirt as well. I sprayed Steam Power Black below the fuel filler neck with an airbrush. If I had this to do over, I would have brush-painted the black so that the edges of the spilled fuel (actually the dust that sticks to the fuel) would be crisp.

After I sprayed the tank with Dirt and Steam Power Black, I drybrushed vertical streaks of Engine Black on the curved face of the tanks, **6**. Dust, dirt, and grime collect on the top and bottom of the tanks, but the vertical faces would be fairly clean. Again, I made sure the streaks of grime were vertical.

I finished weathering the fuel tank by spraying vertical streaks of Railroad Tie Brown and Grimy Black on the ends, roughly in line with the wheels.

Pilots, walkways, and couplers

Though pilots aren't the biggest part of a locomotive, they offer a lot of weathering opportunities, **7**. I started by painting the connections on the m.u. cables Polly Scale ATSF Silver. Then I sprayed the bottom of the pilot with Dirt, the same color I used on the sideframes and fuel tank.

To simulate crud kicked up from trailing locomotives and cars, I sprayed vertical streaks of Railroad Tie Brown in line with the location of the wheels. In hindsight, I probably should have used a color that wasn't so close to Dirt or mixed in some Grimy Black. However, the streaks are visible, which is the effect I was after.

I also had fun weathering the walkways and grab irons. I sprayed the steps and walkways with thinned L&N Gray, which is a versatile weathering color. You can further enhance the steps by

WEATHER WITH AN AIRBRUSH

Though an airbrush is typically associated with painting models, it's also a valuable tool for weathering. Why? Because an airbrush gives you the ability to control air and paint volume (one or both depending on the type of airbrush). These features make it possible to apply weathering coats to large areas and do special-effects techniques like grime streaks and dirt specks.

To weather the Dakota, Minnesota & Eastern (DME) GP40, I used Polly Scale acrylic paints. For regular airbrushing, the manufacturer recommends thinning the paint 10 to 15 percent with distilled water or airbrush thinner. However, for weathering, that formula goes out the window. I generally thin the paint one part paint to four parts 70 percent isopropyl alcohol (distilled water or airbrush thinner will also work). I prefer to build up the weathering colors in light layers. Remember, applying another coat of paint is much easier than cleaning the paint off and starting over.

When weathering, I set the spray pressure between 20 and 30 psi. I also keep a cotton swab soaked in Windex next to the spray booth. I use the cotton swab to clean dried paint off the needle and nozzle between coats.

As with any modeling project, working from prototype photos is ideal. I found photos of

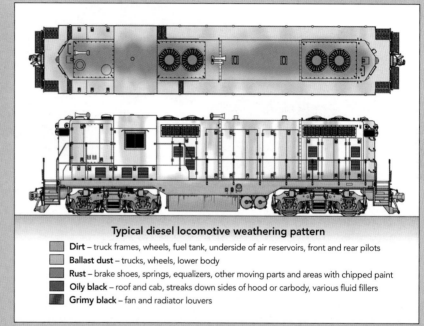

Typical diesel locomotive weathering pattern

■ **Dirt** – truck frames, wheels, fuel tank, underside of air reservoirs, front and rear pilots
■ **Ballast dust** – trucks, wheels, lower body
■ **Rust** – brake shoes, springs, equalizers, other moving parts and areas with chipped paint
■ **Oily black** – roof and cab, streaks down sides of hood or carbody, various fluid fillers
■ **Grimy black** – fan and radiator louvers

Dakota, Minnesota & Eastern GP40s on locophotos.com and rrpicturearchives.net. If you aren't able to find prototype photos, the above illustration is a handy guide for basic locomotive weathering.

Before weathering the DME GP40, I separated the plastic shell from the chassis. Then I removed the cab and carefully popped out the window glazing. I also detached the sill from the hood.

After separating the plastic parts, I washed them in water with a few drops of liquid dish soap. This removed any impurities that might affect paint adhesion.

Once the parts were dry, I was ready to start weathering. I started by spraying the entire shell with three coats of thinned Polly Scale Reefer White, a trick MR's art director Tom Danneman taught me. This gives the vibrant South Dakota State University blue and gold paint a slightly faded look. Apply more coats of thinned white to make the paint look even more sun bleached.

Once all of the weathering colors were applied, I sprayed the entire model with Polly Scale Satin Finish. This not only gives the model a uniform sheen, but it helps protect the weathering.

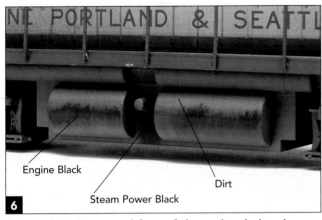

6

Engine Black

Steam Power Black

Dirt

To weather the curved face of the tanks, drybrush on vertical streaks of black.

7

On the pilot, paint the connections on the m.u. cables silver and spray the bottom as done on the sideframes.

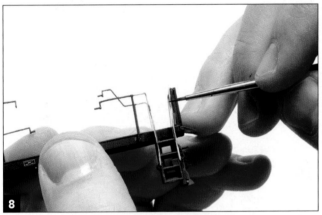

8

To match the prototype look, I randomly drybrushed gray on the vertical portions of the handrails to show where white patches of paint had worn off.

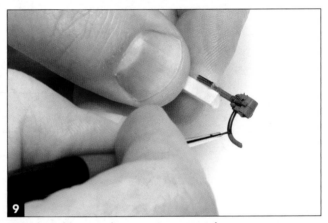

9

Give knuckle couplers a gritty, rusty-brown appearance and then finish by brush-painting the trip pin Grimy Black.

painting the edges white, yellow, silver, or whatever color the prototype used. If you don't have a steady hand for painting the step edges, try using decal stripes, available from several manufacturers.

Next, I turned my attention to the handrails. Many railroads painted the vertical portions of the handrails a contrasting color for safety and visibility. In prototype photos of ex-Spokane, Portland & Seattle units, I noticed that patches of white paint had worn off the vertical portions of the handrails. I replicated that look by randomly drybrushing UP Dark Gray on the verticals, **8**.

Knuckle couplers are small, but when they're weathered, they enhance the overall appearance of a locomotive. To capture that gritty, rusty-brown look of prototype couplers, I mixed one part Polly Scale Dirt and one part Rust. Then I mixed ¼ ounce of mixed paint with ½ ounce of 70 percent isopropyl alcohol and sprayed it with an airbrush.

I applied the paint in thin layers to avoid gumming up the working parts. I finished the couplers by brush-painting the trip pin Grimy Black, **9**.

Some modelers prefer cutting off the trip pin and using body-mounted air hoses. If you do, skip brush-painting the trip pin, but use the same color to paint the air hose castings. Cal-Scale, Details West, and Hi-Tech Details are just some of the manufacturers that offer air hoses in HO scale.

Fans and radiators

Fan and radiator shutters are some of the first places road grime accumulates on the hood of a locomotive. This is particularly noticeable on this yellow SP&S engine.

First, I cut an opening in an index card the same size as the radiator shutters (on this C-425, the shutters

are different sizes, so I had to cut two index cards.) Then I held the stencil on the shell and sprayed the louvers with thinned Polly Scale Steam Power Black, **10**. I used a mixture of 10 drops paint to ½ ounce of 70 percent isopropyl alcohol.

I held the mask in place with my thumb. If you prefer, you can use painter's masking tape (or any low-adhesive tape) to hold the mask in place. It's also a good idea to wear powder-free latex or vinyl gloves to keep the acrylic paint off your hands. If you use organic solvent-based paint, wear nitrile gloves.

The stencil confined the paint to just the radiator shutters, as I intended, **11**. This locomotive was five years old at the time of the BN merger, so I applied a moderate coat of paint to the shutters. A light coat would be sufficient for newer engines; a heavier coat would be appropriate

10 While airbrushing the radiator shutters, hold the mask in place with your thumb or use painter's masking tape.

11 I applied a moderate coat of paint to the shutters as the locomotive was in service for five years.

12 To add scorch marks to the top of the hood doors, I applied thinned Polly Scale Zinc Chromate Primer to the doors with a fine paintbrush.

13 After clear-coating, I applied three coats of a Burnt Sienna wash to the hood, roof, cab, and nose, keeping the brush parallel with the hood doors.

for locomotives that have been in service for many years.

The C-425 has an assortment of areas you can weather this way, including the screens for the dynamic brakes, hood pressurizing fan, and mechanical air cleaner. As always, it's a good idea to work from prototype photos.

Hood, cab sides, and ends

While studying a prototype photo of BN C-425 no. 4253 in Jim Boyd's *Burlington Northern Vol. 2: A Cascade of Color* (Morning Sun Books, 2007), I noticed scorch marks on the tops of the hood doors caused by heat from the dynamic brakes. To re-create this look, I applied thinned Polly Scale Zinc Chromate Primer to the doors with a fine paintbrush, **12**. I put some paint in the jar lid, dipped the brush in distilled water before to touching it to the paint, and then blotted off some paint on a paper towel. Then I brushed the primer

on the doors, following the prototype photo.

After the Zinc Chromate Primer had dried, I sprayed the plastic body shell with Polly Scale Clear Flat. I let the clear coat dry for 24 hours before applying a wash of artist's oils.

I put a small dot of Burnt Sienna into a pallet well. Then I filled the adjacent well with Turpenoid (an odorless turpentine substitute). Next, I dipped a ½"-wide brush into the paint and stirred the brush in the Turpenoid until I'd created a thin wash. I applied three coats of the Burnt Sienna wash to the hood, roof, cab, and nose of the locomotive, keeping the brush parallel with the hood doors, **13**.

Be sure to work in a well-ventilated area when using Turpenoid and follow the manufacturer's instructions. Though Turpenoid can be applied over acrylic paint, it may react with some enamels.

Up on the roof

Though it would be easy to simulate exhaust stains with powdered pastels, I wanted to give it a shot with an airbrush.

I first sprayed the area around the exhaust stack with Steam Power Black, but it didn't pop that much. Then I remembered that Steam Power Black has more gray in it than does Engine Black, so I switched to that color.

After loading the paint jar on my airbrush with Engine Black, I tried simulating the oily soot again. This time, the black paint stood out. I sprayed the paint heaviest around the exhaust stack; thin streaks run down the middle of the hood and feather out over the roof of the cab.

With that, BN C-425 no. 4255 was complete. You can easily adapt these techniques for use on diesel locomotive models based on prototypes built by Electro-Motive Division, General Electric, and other manufacturers.

Re-letter and weather steam engines

1 Class SB 0-8-0 no. 251 was the last steam engine operated by the Virginian Ry. The weathered locomotive, retired in 1957, fits the theme of MR's steam-to-diesel transition model railroad.

When I was given the task of working on 0-8-0 no. 251 for *Model Railroader*'s HO scale Virginian Ry. project layout, I had mixed emotions. Stripping, painting, and decaling a locomotive was no sweat. I've done this countless times. But weathering a steam locomotive was new ground for me. I'm a contemporary diesel guy, and until this point had no reason to weather a steam locomotive. However, the only way I was going to learn was to do it, so off to the spray booth I went.

The Virginian had 15 class SB 0-8-0s (and 20 total 0-8-0s). We selected no. 251 for our locomotive because it was the last steam engine operated by the railroad. Weathering the locomotive to look like it did near its retirement date of June 1, 1957, would fit the theme of our steam-to-diesel transition model railroad, **1**.

Fortunately, I was able to strip the tender, repaint, and decal a Proto 2000 locomotive decorated for the Indiana Harbor Belt with minimal disassembly. Overall, I'm fairly pleased with my first attempt at steam locomotive weathering. The weathering may be a touch on the heavy side, but this is supposed to be a yard engine serving out its last days on the Virginian, so it certainly looks the part. If I had it to do over, I would make the boiler scale and condensation a bit lighter, and probably tone down the rust some.

If you've never re-lettered and weathered a steam locomotive, give it a try. It's a great way to get the locomotive you want for your model railroad and make it look like the real thing.

Stripping the paint

I couldn't find a Virginian 0-8-0, so I stripped the lettering off a locomotive decorated for the Indiana Harbor Belt. Virginian purists will notice that

2 I soaked the tender shell in 91 percent isopropyl alcohol and then gently scrubbed off the herald with a soft-bristle toothbrush. Wear gloves and work in a well-ventilated area during this process.

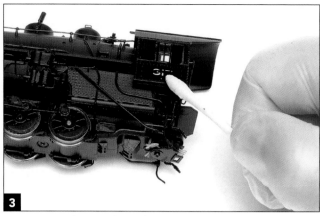

3 To remove the road number and locomotive class lettering from the cab, I used a cotton swab dipped in Pine-Sol, which took several applications.

4 Once the new road number decals slid easily off the backing paper, I positioned them on the cab side with a toothpick and set them.

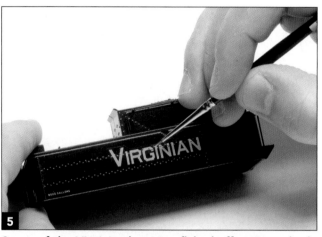

5 Some of the Virginian lettering flaked off, so I touched it up with Polly Scale Seaboard Air Line Yellow, a close match that was not noticeable after weathering.

the locomotive and tender details don't match the full-size no. 251. However, my goal was to produce a plausible stand-in, not a scale replica.

Removing only the large IHB heralds from the tender without damaging the paint or details would have been difficult, so I soaked the shell in 91 percent isopropyl alcohol for 30 minutes. I then used a soft-bristle toothbrush to gently scrub off the paint and lettering, **2**. I used a cotton swab and assorted Microbrushes dipped in the alcohol to remove paint from hard-to-reach areas.

The only lettering on the cab was the road number and locomotive class. Instead of detaching the cab and soaking it in 91 percent isopropyl alcohol, I used a cotton swab dipped in Pine-Sol to remove the lettering, **3**. It took

several applications to remove it all, so I had to be patient. After the lettering was gone, I washed the cab sides with warm water and liquid dish soap to remove any impurities that might affect paint adhesion.

Painting and decaling

The Pine-Sol didn't remove the black paint, so I masked the locomotive and applied Microscale Micro Gloss to the cab side below the windows. The Micro Gloss provides a smooth surface for the decals to adhere to. I let the gloss coat dry for 24 hours before applying the road number decals.

I soaked the decals in distilled water, which is preferable to tap water as it doesn't contain minerals that may dry as white spots. Once the decals slid easily from the backing paper, I

positioned them on the cab side with a toothpick, **4**. I blotted off the excess water with a cotton swab and used Micro Set and Micro Sol decal setting solutions according to the label instructions to soften the decal film and help it conform to the model.

I sprayed the tender with Polly Scale Light Undercoat Gray to ensure that the final color, Polly Scale Steam Power Black, would cover evenly. Once the paint dried (24 hours, or until there is no detectable paint odor), I used an airbrush to apply Micro Gloss. Then I decaled the tender with lettering from Microscale set no. 87-120, Virginian Ry. steam locomotives.

Unfortunately, some of the Virginian lettering flaked off the rivet heads after I applied the decal setting solution. To fix this, I used a paintbrush to carefully

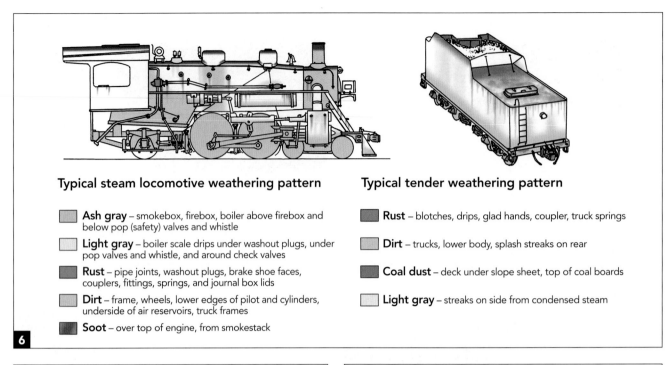

Typical steam locomotive weathering pattern

- ▢ **Ash gray** – smokebox, firebox, boiler above firebox and below pop (safety) valves and whistle
- ▢ **Light gray** – boiler scale drips under washout plugs, under pop valves and whistle, and around check valves
- ▢ **Rust** – pipe joints, washout plugs, brake shoe faces, couplers, fittings, springs, and journal box lids
- ▢ **Dirt** – frame, wheels, lower edges of pilot and cylinders, underside of air reservoirs, truck frames
- ▢ **Soot** – over top of engine, from smokestack

Typical tender weathering pattern

- ▢ **Rust** – blotches, drips, glad hands, coupler, truck springs
- ▢ **Dirt** – trucks, lower body, splash streaks on rear
- ▢ **Coal dust** – deck under slope sheet, top of coal boards
- ▢ **Light gray** – streaks on side from condensed steam

6

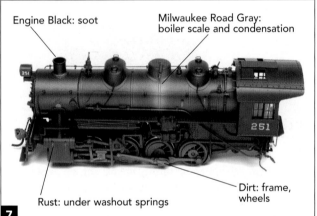

7

Engine Black: soot

Milwaukee Road Gray: boiler scale and condensation

Dirt: frame, wheels

Rust: under washout springs

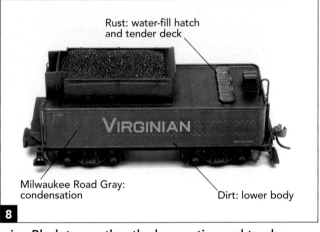

8

Rust: water-fill hatch and tender deck

Milwaukee Road Gray: condensation

Dirt: lower body

I used Polly Scale Milwaukee Road Gray, Rust, Dirt, and Engine Black to weather the locomotive and tender.

apply Polly Scale Seaboard Air Line Yellow, **5**. The color was close to the decal color, but it wasn't an exact match. However, after I weathered the model, the difference was barely noticeable.

Weathering

Prototype photos are the best guide for weathering a steam locomotive. However, photos of steam locomotives aren't always easy to come by, especially in color. However, I did find a color photo of Virginian no. 251 in the *Virginian Railway in Color* (Morning Sun Books, 2005). I also used an illustrated weathering guide (first appeared in MR in August 2002) that provides pointers on how to realistically weather a locomotive and tender, **6**.

Putting it to the test

I used Polly Scale Milwaukee Road Gray, Rust, Dirt, and Engine Black to weather the locomotive and tender, **7** and **8**. I find it best to build up the weathering in light layers. Remember, it's easier to add more weathering than remove too heavy a coat.

After I finished weathering the locomotive and tender, I applied a "control coat" of thinned Polly Scale Tarnished Black (one part paint, one part 70 percent isopropyl alcohol). The control coat tones down and blends the weathering colors and gives the locomotive a more realistic overall finish. Build up the control coat in light layers, as it's easy to obscure the weathering. (I learned

this the hard way.) Also, be sure to mask the headlights, window glazing, and other items you want to remain shiny before applying any of the weathering.

I used an airbrush and paintbrush to apply patches and blotches of Polly Scale Rust on the deck, water-fill hatch, and sides. I added Dirt on the lower body, as well as streaks of Milwaukee Road Gray on the side to suggest condensation. I thinned these colors at one part paint to four parts 70 percent isopropyl alcohol.

Then I sprayed the locomotive and tender with Polly Scale Satin Finish. This protects the weathering, hides the decal edges, and gives the model a uniform satin finish.

9

I separated the tender from the underframe and removed the wheelsets from the trucks. Then I sprayed the underframe with Polly Scale Dirt.

10

Use a Microbrush to paint the wheels and axles Polly Scale Railroad Tie Brown, being careful to keep paint off the axle points so the wheels remain free rolling.

11

To bring out details, I drybrushed the truck sideframes with Polly Scale Milwaukee Road Gray and then painted the leaf springs Rust.

12

With the locomotive drivers spinning on a section of track, I airbrushed thinned Polly Scale Dirt on the drivers, rods, and valve gear.

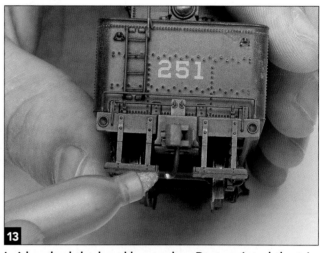

13

I airbrushed the knuckle couplers Rust, painted the trip pin black, and colored the tip of the trip pin silver with a paint marker to suggest a glad hand on the air hose.

Trucks and wheels

I separated the tender from the under-frame and removed the wheelsets from the trucks, **9**. I then masked the printed circuit board and inserted lengths of ³⁄₁₆" styrene tube between the truck and the bolster. This allowed me to easily weather all sides of the trucks. Then I sprayed the underframe with Polly Scale Dirt thinned to the same 4:1 ratio used on the locomotive and tender.

Next, I used a Microbrush to paint the wheels and axles Polly Scale Rail-road Tie Brown, **10**. I was careful to keep paint off the axle points so the wheels would remain free rolling.

After reassembling the tender and reinstalling the wheelsets, I dry-brushed the truck sideframes with Polly Scale Milwaukee Road Gray, **11**. Drybrushing is a technique in which most of the paint is removed from the

brush before it's touched to the model. By lightly touching the brush to the model, it helps bring out raised details and textures.

I painted the leaf springs with Rust. I then painted the bottom of each journal box with Engine Black to suggest a build-up of oil and grease. To make the oil and grease look "shiny," brush on a layer of clear gloss.

Drivers

I put the locomotive and tender on a section of track and attached clip leads from the power pack to the rails, **12**. Holding the tender with my left hand, I airbrushed thinned Polly Scale Dirt on the drivers, rods, and valve gear while letting the drivers spin under power. Using this approach saved me from having to disassemble the entire locomotive.

Try to avoid getting paint on the treads of the drivers. If you do, simply clean the treads with a cotton swab dipped in Windex before the paint dries.

Couplers

I finished the 0-8-0 by airbrushing the Kadee no. 5 knuckle couplers with Polly Scale Rust, **13**. I thinned the paint slightly so the knuckle's spring would still work properly. After the paint dried, I installed the couplers. I then painted the trip pin Polly Scale Tarnished Black and used a paint marker to color the tip of the trip pin silver, which gives the impression of a glad hand on the air hose.

Now Virginian no. 251 is ready to switch the Rogers Yard and pull hoppers up the branch line.

Make couplers look realistic

I've seen many well-weathered models, but too often the effect is ruined by shiny black couplers with bright brass centering springs. But in three easy steps, you can weather your couplers to look more prototypical, **1**.

On my Dakota, Minnesota & Eastern GP40, I wanted the couplers to look older, so I sprayed them with Polly Scale Railroad Tie Brown. Other color options include the firm's Rust (see page 103) and Lifecolor Rust Dark Shadow (6–8 months old). To give the couplers a prototypical finish and to prevent the moving parts from gumming up, I sprayed the paint so it was nearly dry when it hit the coupler.

Before putting my HO scale Dakota, Minnesota & Eastern GP40 into service, I airbrushed the knuckle couplers with acrylic paint.

You can do this by either holding the airbrush farther from the couplers (8" to 10") or using higher air pressure (35-40 psi).

Once the paint dried, I used a Microbrush to paint the trip pins Tarnished Black to simulate the color of a weathered air hose. For a newer coupler, use Engine or Steam Power Black.

I finished the couplers by painting the tips of the trip pins with a silver paint marker to simulate the glad hand.

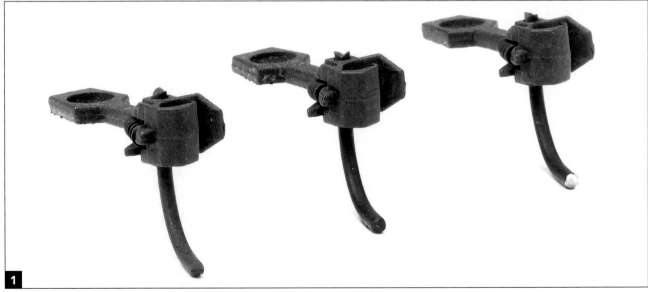

1

The three-step process to realistic knuckle couplers involves painting them Polly Scale Railroad Tie Brown (or your favorite color), painting the trip pin Tarnished Black (this represents an aged air hose), and coloring the tip of the trip pin silver (to suggest the glad hand).

Produce great ghost lettering

1

With its old lettering rusting through the new paint, the Accurail AT&SF three-bay Center Flow covered hopper adds interest to a freight car fleet.

An Accurail AT&SF three-bay Center Flow covered hopper kit was the starting point for this project, **1**. Since I model a Midwest granger shortline railroad, I'm always on the lookout for interesting prototype grain hoppers. One such car that fit that bill was Atchison, Topeka & Santa Fe American Car & Foundry (ACF) three-bay Center Flow covered hopper no. 314671, **2**. The prototype was repainted in the 1990s, but the large Santa Fe billboard lettering from the car's original paint scheme showed through the new paint.

Low-tech stencil

I first sprayed the Accurail model with Polly Scale Mineral Red to cover the factory-applied lettering. I thinned the paint about 35 percent with Polly

Scale Airbrush Thinner to keep it from getting too thick.

Next, I began work on my low-tech stencil. I made two photocopies of the decal-placement guide from Microscale Minical set no. MC-4346 (Santa Fe ACF three-bay covered hoppers). I then taped one of the sheets on a piece of plate glass and cut the stencils using a hobby knife with a fresh no. 11 blade, **3**. The items I made stencils for included the Santa Fe billboard lettering, reporting marks, car capacity data, consolidated lube plates, and notices to close and lock the hopper discharge gates. I also cut a vertical rectangle to represent the automatic car identification labels found on the right end of the hopper. I repeated this process a second time to get stencils for the other side of the car.

I cut the stencils from the paper with scissors, leaving enough room around each stencil for masking tape. I placed the stencils on the car, using my prototype photo as a guide, and held them in place with low-adhesion painter's masking tape (the blue stuff), which doesn't leave adhesive residue on the model.

To the spray booth

To simulate the rusty lettering, I sprayed over the stencils with a blend of Polly Scale Rust and Oily Black, thinned about 50 percent. Once the paint dried, I lightly dusted over it with a mix of Polly Scale Earth, Rust, Oily Black, and Engine Black, thinned as before. I then made one more light pass over the stencils with the Rust and Oily Black to get a mottled look, **4**.

2 Prototype car no. 314671 rolls through Crookston, Minn., in an eastbound unit grain train.

3 To make the stencils, I photocopied the decal-placement guide included with the Microscale set. I placed the paper on a piece of plate glass and used a hobby knife with a sharp no. 11 blade to cut out the letters.

4 After the stencils were removed, I used two different mixes of Polly Scale acrylic paints to give the rusty lettering a mottled look.

I prepared the model for decaling by spraying it with Polly Scale Clear Gloss. I let the clear dry for 24 hours before applying decals from Microscale set no. 87-791 (Santa Fe Quality covered hoppers). This set includes decals for four classes of Santa Fe covered hoppers, but I needed the lettering for only the ACF Center Flow.

Finishing touches

I finished the model by weathering it with my mixture of Oily Black and Rust. Then I used an airbrush to apply a light coat of Polly Scale Mineral Red over the Santa Fe lettering so it would look like it's rusting through in an uneven pattern. Finally, I sprayed the car with Polly Scale Clear Flat.

Before putting my model into service, I installed Kadee no. 5 couplers and 36" metal wheelsets. Now this one-of-a-kind hopper with its ghost lettering is ready to enter service and haul grain throughout the BNSF Ry. system. I look forward to this car being set out in the yard for service on my short line.

CODY SAYS:

Always have a camera handy when you go trackside. You never know when your next project might come rolling by.

Add grime with an airbrush

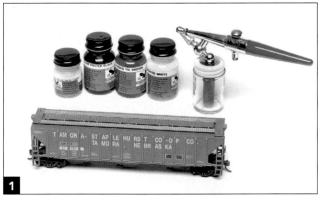

1 You can easily give your freight cars a general coat of grime with an airbrush and thinned acrylic paint.

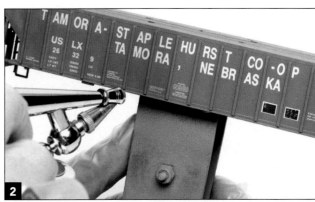

2 I used thinned Polly Scale Reefer White and Railroad Tie Brown to make this covered hopper look faded and dirty. I moved the airbrush in vertical strokes, keeping it parallel with the exterior posts.

3 With the paint still fresh, I used a cotton swab dipped in Windex to remove the weathering coat from the face of each exterior post. Do this carefully so the swab doesn't remove paint from the body panels.

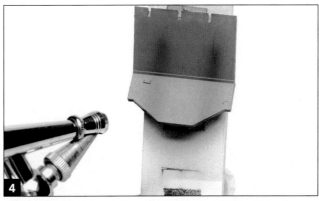

4 Don't forget to weather the ends. I added oil and grease streaks to the slope sheets of the covered hopper with thinned Polly Scale Steam Power Black. The two streaks should be vertical and parallel to each other. The spacing should match the wheel gauge.

If you're looking to give your freight cars and locomotives a general coat of grime in relatively little time, try using an airbrush and thinned acrylic paint, **1**.

My first step on this Athearn HO scale 54-foot covered hopper kit was to spray the entire car with thinned Polly Scale Reefer White (one part paint to nine parts 70 percent isopropyl alcohol). I built up the color in layers, aiming for a slightly faded look.

After the white had dried, I sprayed the car with the same ratio of Polly Scale Railroad Tie Brown. I moved the airbrush in a vertical motion, keeping it parallel with the exterior posts, **2**.

Some of you may be wondering why I recommend using acrylic paints. Well, it's for the next step. After I applied the Railroad Tie Brown, I dipped a cotton swab in Windex and carefully wiped the paint off the faces of the exterior posts, **3**. These posts tend to collect less dirt than the car sides. This subtle bit of reverse weathering is an easy way

to give your exterior-post freight cars some added realism.

I then shifted my attention to the slope sheets, using thinned Polly Scale Steam Power Black to simulate the oil and grease streaks on the car ends, **4**. The key here is to keep the streaks vertical and parallel.

With the weathering complete, I sprayed the carbody with Polly Scale Gloss Finish to prepare for decaling. Afterward, I sprayed the entire model with the firm's Satin Finish.

Apply washes with artist's oils

I used Turpenoid and Burnt Umber oil paint to give the boxcar a weathering wash. Keep the brush parallel with the exterior posts.

I applied blotches of Burnt Umber on the exterior posts to the right of the door and then let the paint dry. This simulates spots where the door has rubbed against the car.

Then I brushed Burnt Sienna on the posts, leaving a halo of Burnt Umber to simulate fresh rust.

After adding rust patches with Burnt Umber and Burnt Sienna, I applied a wash of the latter color to the entire roof.

Artist's oils make it easy to apply weathering washes and simulate rust patches on freight cars, which I did on this HO scale ExactRail boxcar.

First, I put some Burnt Umber on each body panel and on the door. Then, I touched the paint with a ½"-wide paintbrush soaked with Turpenoid (an odorless turpentine substitute). I pulled the thinned paint straight down the car side, keeping the brush parallel to the exterior posts, **1**.

After letting the Burnt Umber wash dry for two hours, I shifted my attention to the exterior posts to the right of the door. When studying prototype photos, I noticed these posts had rust patches where the door had rubbed against them. To simulate this, I first applied blotches of Burnt Umber, **2**. Then I applied Burnt Sienna over the Burnt Umber, leaving a slight halo of the Burnt Umber, **3**.

I used the same techniques to weather the roof, **4**. After the paint had dried, the Burnt Umber and Burnt Sienna looked too vibrant. To remedy this, I applied a Burnt Umber wash, which not only toned down the rust patches but also muted the bright silver. To reduce the chances of removing the rust patches, I applied the wash in a light, almost blotting, motion.

Artist's oils dry slowly, so take your time and be patient. If you don't like how the weathering looks, wipe the paint off with some Turpenoid and try again. This technique is very forgiving.

Weather with powdered pastels

To accentuate the weld seams, I masked them with Post-it notes and applied MIG Productions Cargo Dust pigment with a brush.

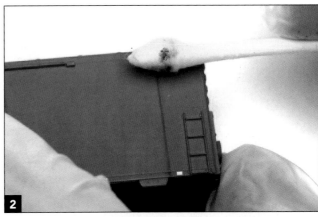

I thought the pigments made the weld seams look too thick, so I removed most of the pigment with a damp cotton swab.

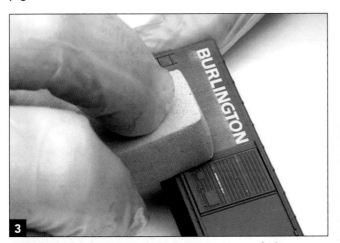

Pastels and a foam sponge make it easy to fade lettering.

I highlighted the springs with Burnt Sienna pastels.

Powdered pastels have long been a popular choice for weathering locomotives, freight cars, and buildings. Several firms offer ready-to-use weathering powders, or you can make your own by scraping pastel sticks with a hobby knife.

I started work on this N scale Micro-Trains boxcar by spraying the entire car with Model Master Lusterless Flat. The flat finish gives the pastels some tooth to bind into.

After the flat finished dried, I began applying MIG Productions Cargo Dust to the weld seams. My hands aren't steady enough to apply the pigment in a straight line, so I used Post-it notes to mask the seams, **1**.

When I removed the masks, I found that the pastels made the weld seams look too thick. I corrected this by wiping off some of the pastels with a damp cotton swab, **2**. I pulled the cotton swab straight down from top to bottom until the streak was more subtle. After I finished all of the weld seams, I sprayed the car with another coat of Lusterless Flat.

To simulated faded lettering, I used a Microbrush to apply PanPastel Titanium White artist's pastels to the bottom of the Burlington lettering. Then, using a Sofft flat sponge bar applicator, I pulled the pastels straight down so the lettering looked chalked and streaked, **3**.

I weathered the truck springs with PanPastel Burnt Sienna, **4**. I then used the same firm's Raw Umber and a Sofft applicator to weather the car roof and ends.

Simulate rust with makeup applicators

I used foam-tipped cosmetic applicators to simulate rust and paint wear on this Athearn HO scale BNSF Ry. SW1000 diesel locomotive.

W hen I asked my wife if we could walk through the cosmetic department at the local drugstore, she gave me a somewhat puzzled look. This part of the store is home to some fantastic weathering tools, including foam-tipped cosmetic applicators. I used these applicators to simulate rust and paint wear on this Athearn HO scale BNSF Ry. SW1000 diesel locomotive.

I started by spraying the entire model with the thinned Polly Scale Reefer White (one part paint to nine parts 70 percent isopropyl alcohol). Since I needed to decal the model, I applied the same firm's Clear Gloss. Once the locomotive was re-lettered, I sprayed the model with Clear Satin.

With the prep work out of the way, I brought out the cosmetic applicators. First, I dipped an applicator in Polly Scale Rust and blotted off most of the color on a paper towel, similar to drybrushing, **1**. Then I gently pressed the

Blot off most of the Polly Scale Rust on a paper towel before gently pressing the applicator to the roof of the switcher. Use the same technique, but with Railroad Tie Brown, to simulate darker rust.

applicator to model, slowly building up the color. Once the Rust dried, I used the same method to apply Railroad Tie Brown. I left a thin halo of the first color to suggest fresh rust.

When studying prototype photos of BNSF 3612, I noticed the locomotive had splotchy patches of grime on the

The full-size switcher had grime on its sills, and you can re-create that look with Railroad Tie Brown and a cosmetic applicator. Set the applicator on the edge of the sill and slowly rock it forward.

sills, **2**. Polly Scale Railroad Tie Brown and a cosmetic applicator was the perfect recipe for re-creating this look on the model.

You could also use this technique to add grime to the front and rear pilots of a locomotive or soot stains on the exhaust stack.

Drybrush different weathering effects

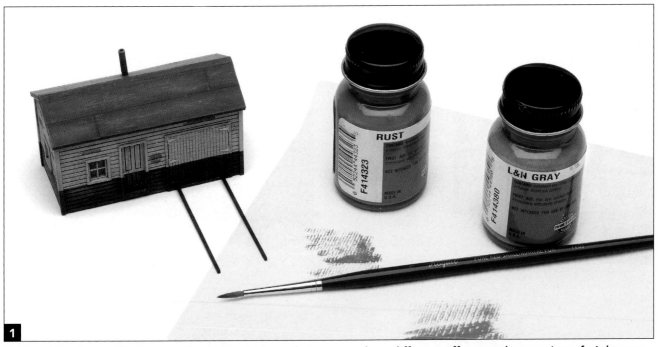

1

Drybrushing is an effective weathering technique that can produce different effects on locomotives, freight cars, and structures such as this HO scale shed.

I've used drybrushing for years on structure roofs, such as this HO scale motor car/work shed produced for the Northern Pacific Ry. Historical Society (nprha.org), **1**.

To drybrush the roof, simply pick up a little paint on a brush, remove all but a trace amount, and gently brush it over the model, **2**. For example, I wanted to make the simulated tarpaper roof on the shed look faded. After preparing a brush with Polly Scale L&N Gray, I began drybrushing. You'll notice in the photo that I'm keeping the brushstrokes parallel to the seams in the roofing material. Avoid wavy lines or those that don't follow natural contours of the model.

But fading roofing material isn't the only effect you can use drybrushing for. I added rust streaks to the base of the vent pipe, **3**. The rust from this pipe is washed down by rain, so the

2

After removing all but a trace amount of Polly Scale L&N Gray from the brush, I began drybrushing the roof on this building, keeping the brush strokes parallel to the seams in the roofing material.

streaks should be vertical, as water flows.

Depending on the size of the model, you may need to reload your brush several times. Before committing your brush to the model, test it

3

Vent pipes and other rooftop items often discolor roofing material. Here, I used Polly Scale Rust to add streaks at the base of this vent pipe. I kept the streaks vertical, as the water would flow.

on an index card or paper towel. Even though the brush may look largely void of paint, there may be some hiding in the interior bristles. I've learned this lesson the hard way on a few models.

Elevate your layout with more expert projects!

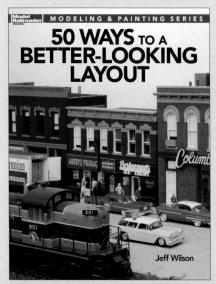